HOT BUTTON
TEACHING SENSITIVE SOCIAL STUDIES CONTENT

29 28 27 26 25 24 23 22   1 2 3 4 5

Published by Gibbs Smith Education
P.O. Box 667
Layton, UT 84041
801.544.9800
www.gibbssmitheducation.com

Publisher: Jared L. Taylor
Editorial Director: Elizabeth Wallace
Managing Editor: Michelle DeVries
Editors: Bart King, Giacomo J. Calabria
Cover design: Dennis Wunsch
Photo Editor: Anna-Morgan Leonards
Copyeditor: Heather Kerrigan

Gibbs Smith books are printed on either recycled, 100% post-consumer waste,
FSC-certified papers, or on paper produced from a 100% certified sustainable
forest/controlled wood source.

Printed and bound in the U.S.A.
ISBN: 978-1-4236-6132-0

CONTENTS

INTRODUCTION

Teaching Social Studies: The Best Hope for Democracy in America

"Facts are stubborn things."
— John Adams, 1770[1]

Educators in the United States are facing a crisis. Our nation's increasingly combative divides, both real and imagined, have damaged our most cherished civic ideals. For example, one in four Americans believe the rioters who attacked the US Capitol in 2021 were "protecting democracy."[2] Almost half the country thinks a second Civil War is likely.[3] Four out of five Americans are worried about the future of democracy at home, never mind abroad.[4] These debates are rapidly changing how effective social studies instruction is researched, taught, and tolerated. Lifelong educators have unjustly lost their jobs.

Books celebrated for teaching painful subjects are being banned from classrooms. History is being rewritten and erased in ways that seriously damage student learning and critical thinking skills.

Why is this happening? Has our shared identity as Americans dissolved? And most important: what can we do about it?

---

1 John Adams, "Adams' Argument for the Defense: 3–4 December 1770," *Founders Online*, National Archives and Records Administration, https://bit.ly/3Iurrfy.

2 "It Was an Attempted Coup: The Cline Center's Coup D'état Project Categorizes the January 6, 2021 Assault on the US Capitol," Cline Center for Advanced Social Research, January 27, 2021, https://bit.ly/3uBtnOR; Brittany Shepherd, "Majority of Americans think Jan. 6 Attack Threatened Democracy: POLL," *ABC News*, January 2, 2022, https://abcn.ws/37ihcgK.

3 William G. Gale and Darrell M. West, "Is the US Headed for Another Civil War?" *Brookings Institution*, September 16, 2021, https://brook.gs/3KwDCJE.

4 Susan Page and Sarah Elbeshbishi, "A Year After Jan. 6, Americans Say Democracy Is in Peril but Disagree on Why: *USA TODAY*/Suffolk poll," USA Today, January 4, 2022, https://bit.ly/3rknaER.

"If destruction be our lot," a 28-year-old Abraham Lincoln warned in 1838, "we must ourselves be its author and finisher. As a nation of freemen, we must live through all time, or die by suicide."[5]

The United States has veered into dangerous waters for a democracy, and nobody knows this better or is more qualified to correct its path than our social studies teachers.

Hot Button was written to help them. It was developed with the understanding that there is no national standard for teaching social studies despite the strong set of skills and practices available to educators. It recognizes that the United States is a vast place with diverse schools and communities.

Our contributors, which include four statewide Teacher of the Year recipients and one National History Teacher of the Year, know that many of the topics they cover are potentially controversial, provocative, and even offensive to some parents and students. These educators are intimately familiar with the myriad of factors that impact a social studies classroom: statewide standards, age appropriateness, curricular materials, wording, past and present controversies, time constraints, emotional hurdles, as well as cutting edge-research and historical discoveries.

This book organizes their decades of experience into six chapters filled with teaching strategies, research, exercises, sample questions, observations, and resources containing readings, handouts, videos, and ready-to-use lesson plans. Taken separately or together, this information will help educators, administrators, department chairs, and teachers-in-training hone their crafts and make the right decisions for their social studies classrooms.

But first, some history.

---

5 Abraham Lincoln, "The Perpetuation of Our Political Institutions: An Address before the Young Men's Lyceum of Springfield, Illinois," January 27, 1838, in Lincoln: Speeches and Writings 1832–1858 (New York: Library of America, 1989), 29.

Understanding Social Studies

Since social studies was first proposed in the early 20th century, its aims were "good citizenship" and contributions to the "social welfare of the community."[6] The field covered civics, economics, and sociology since at least 1905.[7] By 1913, its curricula included US and European history, government, education, human rights, housing, poverty, crime, current events, and even the "impulsive action of mobs."[8] The wide-ranging subject was intended to make students active and informed members of the public, and it also functioned as a guardrail for democracy. Advocates stressed that social studies teachers should inspire students to become lifelong learners, enthusiastic participants in democracy, and pursue ongoing research about the world, which included the successful completion of high school. To quote the educator and sociologist Thomas Jesse Jones (1873-1950):

> The high-school teachers of social studies have the best opportunity ever offered to any social group to improve the citizenship of the land. ... Companions in the schoolroom and on the playgrounds, workers in philanthropy and reform, Government officials and business leaders, voters and laborers of every class are all material for the classroom and laboratory in social studies.[9]

---

6 Thomas Jesse Jones, "Statement of Chairman of the Committee on Social Studies," as quoted in David Warren Saxe, *Social Studies in Schools: A History of the Early Years* (Albany: State University of New York Press, 1991), 182.

7 Edgar Bruce Wesley, *Teaching the Social Studies: Theory and Practice* (New York: D.C. Heath, 1937), 5.

8 Saxe, *Social Studies in Schools*, 182.

9 Saxe, *Social Studies in Schools*, 181–182.

In short, the study of social studies was an American mortar designed to strengthen the nation's citizenry (and by extension, their government) brick by brick.[10] Yet while good education in history and civics is ideally supposed to stave off decay, some might argue that facts are not as stubbornly reliable or easy to spot as they were when John Adams was still a lawyer. Approximately 95 percent of adults in the United States view the spread of misinformation as a problem.[11]

The public's trust in scientists, journalists, elected officials, and public school principals is in steep decline.[12] Highly dedicated teachers and administrators are at risk of losing their jobs over manufactured conspiracies or broadly misunderstood theories. In the outcry over Critical Race Theory (CRT), state legislators began banning its instruction despite the fact that CRT was not in their own state standards. In some states, discussing race or racism was so fraught, hotlines were established to report educators attempting to teach about race issues.[13] Additionally, young citizens are so easily lured toward disinformation on "civic issues" that a Stanford study described the situation as "dismaying," "bleak," and a "threat to democracy."[14] These are the very ills that a social studies education is supposed to cure.

Yet shortly after the passage of the No Child Left Behind Act of 2001, 36 percent of school districts reduced the time they dedicated to social studies. This resulted in the net loss of approximately one month of social studies coverage per academic year.[15] Although the act was repealed in 2015, one social studies teacher noted, its impact is evident in colleges "when students in a 100-level history course do not understand the difference between primary and

---

10 Saxe, *Social Studies in Schools*, 200.

11 Billy Morgan, "Pearson Institute/AP-NORC Poll: 95% of Americans Say the Spread of Misinformation Is a Problem," Harris School of Public Policy, October 11, 2021, https://bit.ly/3JC21vY.

12 Brian Kennedy, Alec Tyson, and Cary Funk, "Americans' Trust in Scientists, Other Groups Declines," Pew Research Center, February 15, 2022, https://pewrsr.ch/3xoDMz4.

13 Chris Kahn, "Many Americans Embrace Falsehoods about Critical Race Theory," *Reuters*, July 15, 2021, https://reut.rs/3jsw4fc.

14 Stanford History Education Group, "Evaluating Information: The Cornerstone of Civic Online Reasoning," Stanford University, November 22, 2016, https://stanford.io/38EJ8f7.

15 Jen Kalaidis, "Bring Back Social Studies," *The Atlantic*, September 23, 2013, https://bit.ly/3KzXjQM.

secondary sources, ... or when students in upper-level courses have trouble identifying and evaluating a historian's argument."[16]

Put simply, social studies has been a "disappearing curriculum" throughout the 21st century.[17] And the declining number of college students pursuing degrees in the humanities—particularly education—presents yet another challenge for our overworked, underpaid, and exhausted educators.[18]

A Look Inside *Hot Button*

Preserving social studies requires concerted, continuous efforts by every level of the country that the field of study was intended to protect. Since social studies is such a vast, important, and under-prioritized subject, this book will focus primarily on who we believe need our help the most: our teachers. If you want to know how an award-winning educator taught class for students minutes away from the US Capitol on January 6, 2021, turn to Alysha Butler-Arnold's courageous account and insight into "Teaching about Domestic Terrorism in Real Time" (Chapter 1). Readers interested in how to teach sensitive social studies topics to young students will be interested in Nicole Butler-Hooton's inspired contribution. Oregon's 2021 Teacher of the Year will provide you with the best methods, resources, and guidance so that you too may "Be the Change Our Students Need" (Chapter 2).

Gerardo Muñoz, Colorado's 2021 Teacher of the Year, recreates everything from his master's classes to his celebrated approach and podcast in his introspective examination of "Roads Untraveled" (Chapter 3). He is followed by curriculum specialist Kelly Reichardt, who shares the best activities and handouts she designed when using primary sources to teach delicate social studies subjects (Chapter 4).

---

16 Samantha Stearns, "'What Changed' in Social Studies Education: A View from the Classroom," *Perspectives on History* (blog), American Historical Association, July 30, 2019, https://bit.ly/3rnkO8i.

17 Margit E. McGuire, "What Happened to Social Studies?: The Disappearing Curriculum," Phi Delta Kappan 88, no. 8 (April 2007): 620–24, https://bit.ly/3M0yRsg; Sheree Turner, "The Disappearing Social Studies Curriculum (and Tips to Integrate Content into Other Subjects!)," Social Studies School Service (blog), SocialStudies.com, January 22, 2020, https://bit.ly/3E8UBPG.

18 Michael T. Nietzel, "Whither the Humanities: The Ten-Year Trend In College Majors," *Forbes*, January 7, 2019, https://bit.ly/3O6OgZH.

For readers interested in ready-to-use lesson plans on state-sponsored genocide, turn to Leah Voit's expansive interview with Jennifer Wolfe, New York State's 2021 Teacher of the Year (Chapter 5). Finally, for a vast selection of experiences and philosophies to teaching social studies, turn to the "Shared Perspectives" collected by Brooke Brown, Washington's 2021 Teacher of the Year, and the experts she assembled from across the country (Chapter 6).

In addition to these essays, there is also a selection of readings and handouts provided in this book's Appendix.

The editors are proud to have worked with such an outstanding team of contributors. They took time from their busy schedules to provide the best tools, methods, and insight they have to offer. We thank them for their hard work, their tireless dedication to their students, and for the wisdom they have shared.

CHAPTER 1

Insurrection Nation: Teaching About Domestic Terrorism in Real Time

Alysha Butler-Arnold
Washington, DC

On January 6, 2021, the United States suffered what Federal Bureau of Investigation Director Christopher Wray deemed an act of "domestic terrorism," and what numerous researchers and members of Congress considered a "coup attempt." For five hours, the US Capitol was besieged by a violent mob determined to prevent the transfer of power from one president to the next. Dozens of rioters came armed with deadly weapons, and one even paraded a Confederate flag within the building. This was something that had not happened at any time in US history, even during the Civil War.

As the nation watched the attack unfold, teachers like Alysha Butler-Arnold, whose school is only two miles away from the Capitol, faced the added challenge of keeping their students safe while explaining what was happening to their country. Butler's article recounts her experience of what happened that day, and also documents her approach to teaching about racism, domestic terrorism, and US history.

Hope Deferred

On January 6, 2021, I began my workday with hope and fervor. This emotion was quite different from how I began the school year just a few months prior, when the COVID-19 pandemic led to the abrupt closure of schools across the country. Teachers were instructed to reconfigure their methods for an entirely virtual platform. We had to somehow offer the same level of quality instruction and student engagement as in-person learning. We were also expected to meet the social and emotional needs of many students we had never met. At the same time, we struggled to care for the physical and mental well-being of our own families during a health crisis that had brought the United States and the rest of the world to a halt.

However, January 6, 2021, was a special day.

I was closely watching the two US Senate races in Georgia. Regardless of one's political affiliation, showing students real-life cases of people making history and becoming "firsts" both energizes and motivates a classroom. With all the police brutality and official misconduct my students witnessed around the country and in their own city in 2020, they were understandably cynical. They did not believe that Rev. Raphael Warnock had a chance in the Georgia special election, but the previous day, I told them to keep a close eye on the outcome. Classes would not be held on January 6 because Wednesdays were designated asynchronous days, so I wanted my students prepared to discuss the results when classes resumed the next day.

When Warnock was indeed declared the winner, I could not wait to use his victory as an example of how our vote matters. It was and remains a real-life example of how people could still make a difference in this country, no matter their ethnicity, age, education, sexual orientation, or socioeconomic background. The fact that the son of a woman who spent countless backbreaking hours picking cotton in the Jim Crow South was now the first Black man elected to represent Georgia in the US Senate could make even the most ardent cynic of modern politics a believer. The fact that this happened despite the then-president's baseless and racially motivated accusations of voter fraud—aimed primarily at large metropolitan areas with strong concentrations of Black voters— further enshrined my point that people who look like my primarily Black and Latinx students can make a change.

January 6 was supposed to be one of those days where teachers would forget the many hours of unpaid work, the instances they had to dip into their own meager funds for essential classroom supplies, or the numerous times they have been the lone scapegoat for students' failure to meet the unreasonable demands of flawed standardized assessments. It should have been one of those moments that reminded us why we became teachers. Although days like these are not always as abundant as teachers would like, January 6 was going to be *my* day.

Instead, my hope turned to horror as I watched the invasion of the US Capitol by Confederate flag-waving rioters chanting for the lynching of the vice president while trashing, looting, and defiling the site where historic legislation—like the Voting Rights Act of 1965, which enabled Warnock's victory—had been debated and passed.

I wrestled with what I was going to say to my students the next day. Unlike most of America's teachers, my students lived within walking distance of the Capitol Rotunda. Most of them reside in a place once proudly nicknamed "Chocolate City." They watched a mob of white outsiders wave Confederate flags—and in some cases, carry nooses—on the same routes they walked to school. This forced them to question their physical safety in their own backyard—and in their own country.

Unlike teachers in the rest of the nation, I had to prepare a lesson that first gave them a safe forum to express how they felt, to comfort them, and to let them know that they were safe. I emphasized that the strength of our democratic republic relies on individuals like them not allowing mob rule or political demagogues to deter them from voting, or to discount the legitimacy of their votes. I cannot remember the last time in my 22-year teaching career when I was so emotionally charged, determined, and scared.

As a social studies teacher, I knew that my students were looking to me for clarity amid the crisis the same way that my friends and family members were.

The next day, I found my hope restored through discussions with some of my current and former students. While they may have been confused that this happened in 2021, unlike much of the mainstream media and American public, my students were not left asking how this could happen in the United States of America.

For months after the insurrection, I was shocked, angered, and exhausted by the constant bombardment of op-eds and articles with titles like "This Is Not America," "America Hit Rock Bottom on January 6," and "January 6th and the Crime of the Century." My students were already able to grasp, interpret, and contextualize what they had witnessed that day. They returned to class with a renewed energy to engage in the type of discourse that national standardized and college preparatory tests blindly try and fail to assess. They were prepared to apply the history that they had been learning to a real world shaken by a life-changing event.

In short, my students were ready and able because I had done my job as a history teacher: I made room in my curriculum to explore a more complete, honest, and complicated history of this nation.

Setting a Purpose-Driven Classroom and Curriculum

If you walk into my classroom, you will be greeted by a poster on the door featuring writer and activist James Baldwin, along with a variation of his famous observation: "People are trapped in history and history is trapped in them."[1] You will then come across an easel in the middle of the room with an old African proverb which states, "Until the lion becomes the historian, the hunter will always be the hero." It is the first item to go up in my class before the school year starts and the last to come down for summer break. On the very first day of every school year, in lieu of the typical get-

1 James Baldwin, "Stranger in the Village," *Harper's Magazine,* October 1953, 42–48.

to-know-you icebreakers, my students get to know each other as we dissect and discuss the proverb.

At the end of our discussion, I inform all my students that the proverb will be our classroom motto for the year. Everything we learn in class will be interpreted and evaluated under the guidance of that motto. I let them know that they are in training for how to pursue and uncover the lion's story in every historical event. Along the way, they might find out that we're not entirely sure where that proverb comes from. The lion's work, much like the teacher's and historian's, is ongoing.

My desire to tell a more comprehensive narrative of this country has been the driving force behind my 22-year teaching career.

I was fortunate to grow up with three generations of family members within a 20-mile radius in Hallandale, Florida. Sunday dinners were rich with tales: of my great-grandfather, a Bahamian immigrant who dodged the Klan as a rum-runner smuggling alcohol into Coconut Grove during the Great Depression; of my grandfather, who served in a segregated regiment as a Marine during World War II; and of my father, who was among the second generation of Black students who bravely integrated the local high school.

Their stories made my surroundings come alive, and in time, I realized that Baldwin's words were true. My parents, grandparents, and great-grandparents were living and breathing examples of history, and I was fortunate to see my surroundings through their eyes. But none of their stories were ever present in the textbooks I read or the classroom lectures I heard. To this day, I still struggle to understand whether this was a result of my teachers' ignorance or if it was a deliberately chosen silence. I promised myself to make the unheard voices in history, the stories of marginalized and silenced groups, the center of my curriculum when I became a teacher.

Although state curriculum standards have served as the base of my teaching, over the years I have attempted to fill in any gaps or holes that were conveniently omitted. For example, most school districts around the country are mandated to cover the 1920s, which are usually framed in a way to help students understand the economic, social, and political behaviors that led to the Great Depression. The era's nickname of the "Roaring Twenties" suggests it was a period dominated by wild parties, irresponsible financial behavior, and an enabling federal government. This description leaves little room to explore why the late, great actress Cicely Tyson stated in her memoir *Just As I Am*: "In white America, the '20s may have roared, but in my Black world . . . the decade also moaned." I can only imagine that Tyson was evoking events many Black people of her time witnessed, like the 1920 Ocoee Massacre in Orlando, Florida.

The killings took place when Moses Norman, a Black man from Ocoee, had the audacity to exercise his 15th Amendment right to vote.[2] After he was turned away for refusing to pay a $1 poll tax, a deputized mob of white supremacists attacked the home of a Black man named Julius Perry, ostensibly because they believed he was harboring Norman. Descendants of the survivors of the massacre claimed that Perry was targeted because he was prosperous and had worked to register other Blacks in the area.

After wounding members of Perry's family in a shootout, Perry was captured, brutalized, and later publicly lynched to serve as a warning to other Black people who threatened the political power of the local white supremacist establishment. The white mob also attacked and set fire to the rest of the neighborhood in an event later known as the Election Day Massacre. About two dozen Black homes were burned, as well as two churches and a fraternal lodge. The total number of people killed is still unknown. Many Black residents fled the town, leaving their lives and property behind, never to return.

Despite the fact that many family members alive today still feel the human and financial loss of the Ocoee Massacre, it was not until 2020 that the state of Florida mandated that the tragic event be taught in schools.[3] For the previous century, most Floridians, myself included, who had gone through the state's school system

2 Stephen Hudak, "Story of Ocoee Massacre Finally Being Told -100 Years After It Happened," *Orlando Sentinel*, October 30, 2020, https://bit.ly/3Ee6iEX.

3 Kimberly Wilson, "Florida Schools Now Must Teach the Ocoee Election Day Massacre. Here's Why That Matters," *Tampa Bay Times*, June 25, 2020, https://bit.ly/3LVopCg.

had never heard of the horrifying election violence that devastated a community just 10 miles from what is now Cinderella's castle at Disney World.[4]

What happened in Ocoee was not an isolated event. More than 20 years earlier, Wilmington, North Carolina, a once unique and progressive city, was similarly stained with racial violence. What makes Wilmington's 1898 tragedy different from any other is that it marked the only incident in the post-Reconstruction South where a legitimately elected government was overthrown in a white supremacist *coup d'état*.

During Reconstruction (1865–1877), Wilmington enjoyed a 56 percent Black majority, with a sizable Black middle class and police force, and was home to a multiracial government where Blacks, Republicans, and white Populists worked together. It was an extremely rare success story in the post-Reconstruction era, but even it was not free from the resentment of white supremacists.

During the 1898 municipal election, white militia groups and a statewide racist organization called the Red Shirts stockpiled military-style weapons and spread false rumors about Black sexual assaults and a Black insurgency. The groups also launched a coordinated campaign to intimidate Black voters, take over Wilmington, and to put an end to the city's so-called "negro rule."

On November 10, the insurgents successfully overthrew the city's government by force. The white mob forced all Black politicians to resign and issued a White Declaration of Independence. A riot ensued days later when Black men attempted to defend themselves from ongoing physical attacks. More than 2,000 Blacks were driven out of the city, and at least 60 Blacks were killed. When the dust settled, the city's Black population had dropped from 56 percent to 18 percent, a change from which it has never fully recovered. Democratic-sponsored laws disenfranchised Black men, bringing an end to an era of Black participation in Wilmington politics.

While the *coup* did not go unnoticed nationally, there was no federal intervention. President William McKinley (himself once an

---

4Ibid.

abolitionist and Union officer in the Civil War) feared disrupting the nation's unified mood after its recent victory in the Spanish-American War. As a result, President McKinley failed to even comment on the Wilmington coup.[5]

Connecting the Dots

Neither the Ocoee Massacre nor the Wilmington Coup are included in my curriculum as a teacher, yet both are essential components for a complete understanding of life in America after the Civil War. More importantly, learning about both of these American tragedies proved essential for my students to effectively process the January 6 insurrection, and were referenced in my conversations with them.

So when a mob of overwhelmingly white Americans tried to throttle the voices of a diverse electorate that included Black and Brown citizens who were driven by hope for equal opportunity, my students had a basis of historical comparison. When the January 6 rioters unleashed violence because they refused to accept any threat to their power, it was not hard for my students to understand. They had already learned about what had happened in Ocoee and in Wilmington. Furthermore, my students did not fall into the convenient and lazy trap of interpreting the US Capitol insurrection as an outlier in our nation's history. Because I had extensively covered Reconstruction and all its failures, they knew the January 6 riot was a part of this country's penchant for using violence to settle political disputes.

Reconstruction lasted from the end of the Civil War to 1877. In an approximately 12-year period, formerly enslaved African Americans became free citizens, with Black men being promised the right to vote. Yet nearly as soon as the right to vote was granted, it was snatched from more than a half million Black voters due to new state laws written by white supremacists in the South.

---

5 Dave Davies, "'Wilmington's Lie' Author Traces The Rise Of White Supremacy In A Southern City," *NPR*, January 13, 2020, https://n.pr/3LVDSlK.

Reconstruction was also a period of horrific racial violence against Black people in the South where massacres "were frequently waged by mobs seeking to brutally suppress the Black vote or to instill fear and terror in the entire Black community by killing alleged 'suspects' accused of unproven offenses."[6] According to the Equal Justice Initiative, there were more than 2,000 lynchings of Black people during this period. Many experts believe the actual number is much higher, because victims sometimes went missing and their deaths were never documented for fear of retaliation.[7] According to historian David Blight, one of the leading experts on race and racism after Reconstruction:

> This is a part of American history that isn't easy to face. It tells us that we had a moment in our history when our politics broke down, our society broke down, our police power broke down; the government wasn't functioning sufficiently enough to protect one group of citizens from another who simply engaged in wanton vigilante violence of the worst kind.[8]

Simply put, it was a uniquely racial, political, and humanitarian disaster. It was American exceptionalism of the worst kind, and it is forever etched in the history we have to teach.

Filling in the Holes

The period of hope and terror from the Civil War to today is still largely overlooked or minimized in state curricula across the country. This became clear to me three months prior to the January 6 insurrection, when I agreed to teach a virtual class on Selma and the Voting Rights Act of 1965 for the Gilder Lehrman Institute of

6 Equal Justice Initiative, "Documenting Reconstruction Violence," in Reconstruction in America: Racial Violence after the Civil War, 1865–1876, (Montgomery, AL: Equal Justice Initiative, 2020), https://bit.ly/3LTLJQK.

7 Ibid.

8 David Blight, "Southern Violence During Reconstruction," interview by PBS Online/WGBH Boston, July 30, 2018, first published December 19, 2003, https://to.pbs.org/3rknRxX.

American History. I accepted the invitation with some hesitation, for I had barely survived teaching virtually during the lockdown months of 2020 with the students with whom I had already built a rapport. Teaching this class meant I would have more than 100 students from different states and educational backgrounds on a virtual platform I still found myself stumbling with.

I could not, however, walk away from the opportunity. The country was steeped in racial tension that summer. Many Americans were mourning the death of Ahmaud Arbery, Breonna Taylor, and George Floyd. People and students were looking for answers to help them process these public tragedies.

I began the class with a comprehensive lesson on Reconstruction. At the end of the class, my students were tasked with constructing a reflection where they detailed what they learned, how the information challenged or reaffirmed their existing knowledge on Reconstruction, and why they thought more people should be educated on the subject. One response from a young female student from New York really let me know just how neglected Reconstruction is in school systems. She wrote:

> One fact that I learned from the presentation was how Reconstruction was not peaceful, but a period of fierce opposition to the few rights that the African American community had just received. My 8th grade U.S. History course only covered up to the Civil War, so I am rather ignorant on Reconstruction onward. I always thought that the Emancipation Proclamation was the "end all, be all" for institutional inequality. Of course, I know that institutional racism exists and has for the past century, but it has always been drilled into my brain that the Civil W[ar] earned all racism that a government could express toward a single group of people. Consequently, I subconsciously thought that oppression stopped during Reconstruction and magically materialized in time for the Civil Rights movement of 1964. Therefore, this presentation's

lesson on Reconstructions challenged my pre-existing
belief that the Civil War ended institutional racism.

Here was a student who had attended a well-equipped high school in a "post-racial" society, but who had absolutely no knowledge of an essential part of US history or its attendant racial politics.

Her experience sadly mirrored my own. Throughout my junior high and high school years in Florida, I had never heard or been taught anything related to Reconstruction. Like her, I was simply told that President Abraham Lincoln freed the slaves. There were no subsequent discussions on their fates or the post-war lives of Black citizens until we approached the civil rights era, which was treated by my teachers as a footnote before a thorough exploration of the Ronald Reagan years. I would not learn about Reconstruction until I attended college.

When I surveyed my own 11th grade high school students in 2020 and 2021, I found a few similarities in their familiarity with the subject. Only 55 percent of my students had even heard of Reconstruction, and 73 percent of those who did spent less than a week discussing it with their instructors. By the end of the school year, 100 percent of those surveyed considered Reconstruction a key component for understanding modern-day race relations, with 78 percent deeming it "very important" and 22 percent choosing "moderately important."

It can be difficult to get any student to acknowledge the necessity in learning a new skill or topic. Perhaps my students understand Reconstruction's importance because they clearly see its parallels in modern events. Our students currently live in a country where white supremacist militia groups brazenly carry military-style weapons in the open alongside Confederate iconography. They parade these weapons and hateful symbols into town halls and state buildings, like in Michigan, with the sole intention of intimidating legislators to vote in their favor.[9] They live in a country where different forms of voter disenfranchisement exist in almost all 50 states, and where the only difference between the Black victims of white supremacy in 1898 and today is the open alliance they enjoy with a former president of the United States. The federal government turned a blind eye to the Wilmington insurrection when it happened. In the 21st century, the federal government under the Trump administration was often accused of slyly winking at white supremacists without giving them overt support.[10]

Can there be any doubt that if more white Americans had learned about Reconstruction and events like the Wilmington Massacre, they would not have subsequently been shaking their heads in disbelief? Naturally, I am not suggesting that this be the only aspect of America's history taught in classrooms. I am simply reporting that Reconstruction and its consequences are far too prominent in the world today for our curriculum and textbooks to mitigate or omit. I understand that teachers who read this essay might agree with Reconstruction's impact but simply do not have the time to cover it in full. I argue that the best remedy is teaching with purpose. For example, I use my unit on Reconstruction to teach general concepts, such as voter disenfranchisement, while providing poignant examples from US history that have lasting power. These will motivate students to vote after they leave my classroom, and the Colfax Massacre is one of the strongest—and most awful—examples imaginable.

---

9 Abigail Censky, "Heavily Armed Protesters Gather Again At Michigan Capitol To Decry Stay-At-Home Order," *NPR*, May 14, 2020, https://n.pr/38MPbyv.

10 Vern E. Smith, "Trump's Wink Toward White Supremacism Raises the Age-Old Question: Which Side Are You On?" *Yahoo!* News, October 7, 2020, https://yhoo.it/3JNyuQp; Paul LeBlanc, "Elizabeth Warren: Trump Should Not 'Wink and Nod and Smile' About White Supremacy," *CNN*, August 4, 2019, https://cnn.it/3O5arQ4; Ed Mazza, "Livid Van Jones Rages Against Trump's 'Wink And A Nod' To Nazis During Debate," *HuffPost*, September 30, 2020, https://bit.ly/3jstyWi.

The Colfax Massacre and January 6

The early 1870s were a tumultuous time in Louisiana history. The 1872 governor's race was extremely close between Republican candidate William Kellogg and Democratic candidate John McEnery. After Kellogg won, Louisiana's Democrats refused to acknowledge the election as legitimate. President Ulysses S. Grant was forced to send federal troops to support Kellogg, and a federal judge eventually had to seat him in office, along with other Republican-friendly candidates.

In response, white supremacists organized a group called the White League in order to intimidate potential Black voters.[11] Some residents in Grant Parish were concerned that the Democrats would interfere in their local elections, so Black volunteers organized a militia and seized the courthouse. Then more than 150 whites led by former Confederate soldiers, Klan members, and the White League surrounded the courthouse with weapons, including rifles and a cannon. Fighting erupted on April 13, 1873, and the Black militia was forced to surrender. It is believed that anywhere between 60 and 150 Black men and three white men were killed that day. Although dozens of Black men were killed in battle, the remaining were slaughtered later that day after they surrendered.

In the aftermath of the massacre, only nine of the 97 indicted white residents were charged with an official crime of violating the Enforcement Acts of 1870 and 1871. The Enforcement Acts (also known as the Klan Acts) were a series of laws meant to protect the rights of the formerly enslaved:

> The first law prohibited voter discrimination and banned the use of terror to prevent people from voting on account of their race. The second law put federal elections under federal supervision in Southern states under military rule. The third law broadened President Grant's powers to enforce these laws.[12]

---

11 Danny Lewis, "The 1873 Colfax Massacre Crippled the Reconstruction Era," *Smithsonian Magazine*, April 13, 2016, https://bit.ly/3rko4Bf.

12 NPS, "Protecting Life and Property: Passing the Ku Klux Klan Act," September 6, 2021, https://bit.ly/3KBYD5P.

The prosecutors decided to pursue charges of conspiracy. The case was sent to the Supreme Court, which overturned the lower courts' decisions, arguing that the Enforcement Acts applied only to states, not to individuals.[13] The Colfax murderers walked free without even a slap on their wrists.

When I cover the Colfax Massacre and Reconstruction in class, I do not introduce their tragedies in isolation, while referencing nameless Black victims for shock value. Instead, I first explore the different aspects of congressional Reconstruction and acknowledge the political advances Blacks made on the heels of the 15th Amendment.

A concrete way of doing this is by reviewing the 1872 lithograph by Currier and Ives.[14] This visual depicts Black legislators who were elected to the 41st and 42nd U.S. Congress. I especially enjoy having the students analyze this image and answering questions such as "How are the men portrayed?" and "Based on their demeanor, what assumptions can you make regarding their character or intellect?" More importantly, I ask students how many of them have ever seen Black men portrayed with such pride and dignity in Civil War or Reconstruction documents.

Next, I have students analyze and compare the way Black senators are portrayed in Currier and Ives' 1872 lithograph with "Colored Rule in a Reconstructed State," a political cartoon from 1872 by Thomas Nast.[15] I ask the students:

1. How are Black Americans portrayed differently in this political cartoon by Thomas Nast?
2. If you were ignorant of Reconstruction, what assumptions would you make about Congressional Reconstruction based on Nast's depiction?

---

13 Lewis, "The 1873 Colfax Massacre Crippled the Reconstruction Era."

14 Currier and Ives, "The First Colored Senator and Representatives - in the 41st and 42nd Congress of the United States," lithograph, 1872, Library of Congress Prints and Photographs Division, https://bit.ly/3O6fkZ9. See Appendix I, in the back of this book.

15 Thomas Nast, "Colored Rule in a Reconstructed(?) State," *Harper's Weekly*, March 14, 1874, p. 229, from 1872, Library of Congress Prints and Photographs Division, https://bit.ly/3rlN3nz.

3. How do these different depictions of Reconstruction help counter or support our class motto, "Until the Lion becomes a historian, the hunter will always be the hero"?

After we finish our image analysis, I explain to the students that, unfortunately, Nast's image had been used to illustrate Black political participation in Reconstruction instead of the Currier and Ives' 1872 lithograph for many years.[16]

We next read a short excerpt from Eric Foner's article "Rooted in Reconstruction: The First Wave of Black Congressmen."[17] Students discuss how and why the images and information in the texts challenge or reaffirm their previous assumptions about Black political participation during Reconstruction. I then have my class examine portraits of Black senators currently serving in Congress, along with a graph of Black congressional membership since Reconstruction.[18] The graph shows that by 1901, the number of Blacks serving in Congress dropped from 16 members to zero.

When my students demand an explanation for low Black political participation post-Reconstruction, I describe the different methods of voter suppression (such as the poll tax, grandfather clause, and literacy tests). I also turn our attention to the Colfax Massacre. For in-class work or homework, I have everyone read excerpts from Danny Lewis's 2016 article "The 1873 Colfax Massacre Crippled the Reconstruction Era," and two primary

---

16 Something worth mentioning to students is Nast's prominence in political cartooning and US popular culture from the mid-nineteenth century onward. His iconic use of Santa Claus during the Civil War, for example, should surprise most students while demonstrating how even those supportive of the Union effort could still be racist. For more, see Ronald G. Shafer, "The First Modern Santa Claus Was a Civil War Hero," *Washington Post*, December 23, 2021, https://wapo.st/3xjjTte; and Lorraine Boissoneault, "A Civil War Cartoonist Created the Modern Image of Santa Claus as Union Propaganda," *Smithsonian Magazine*, December 19, 2018, https://bit.ly/3Ju2oc4.

17 Eric Foner, "Rooted in Reconstruction: The First Wave of Black Congressmen," *The Nation*, October 15, 2008, https://bit.ly/3xmvdVr.

18 Library of Congress, Congressional Research Service, Ida A. Brudnick and Jennifer E. Manning, African American Members of the U.S. Congress: 1870–2020, RL30378, (2020), 6, https://bit.ly/3KDDc4a.

source accounts on the massacre from the 19th century.[19] Students use the readings in small groups to construct a cause-and-effect timeline of the events leading up to the massacre.

Students later participate in a Paideia seminar using the documents they read throughout the lesson as reference.[20] Its open-ended questions center on asking whether the ideals expressed in the Declaration of Independence were realized by 1876, and to what extent white supremacy and violence have shaped or hindered American democracy.

Since the events of the January 6 US Capitol riot, I have altered the lesson. The next time I teach my Reconstruction unit, my students will construct a Venn diagram to better understand similarities in the causes of both the 1873 Colfax Massacre and January 6 insurrection. Then I'll ask them to analyze the video footage and images of the Confederate flag on display in the Capitol, as well as the makeshift gallows erected on the National Mall.

We will read interviews and tweets from former President Donald Trump in which he demanded the disenfranchisement of thousands of Black men and women from those metropolitan cities that cost him the election.[21] We will listen to the speech Trump's political allies gave immediately before the attack, which encouraged the rioters to "walk down to the Capitol" and "fight

---

19 Lewis, "The 1873 Colfax Massacre Crippled the Reconstruction Era"; "Condition of the South," Report Number 261, in Reports of Committees of the House of Representatives for the Second Session of the Forty-Third Congress (Washington D.C.: U.S. Printing Office, 1875), pp. 11–14, https://goo.gl/fsC5mu; Committee of 70, "History of The Riot at Colfax, Grant Parish, Louisiana, April 13th, 1873: With a Brief Sketch of the Trial of The Grant Parish Prisoners In The Circuit Court Of The United States" (New Orleans: Clark & Hofeline, 1874), 1, 4, 5, 6, 7, 8, 10–11, 12, 13; from Scott Yenor, ed., "Colfax Massacre Reports," TeachingAmericanHistory.org, https://bit.ly/3O66qeo.

20 A collaborative intellectual dialogue about a text, facilitated with open-ended questions.

21 As Donald Trump's Twitter account @realDonaldTrump was suspended, educators can rely on screenshots of these tweets. For this exercise, I recommend those found in images 11 and 12 of Anna Sakellariadis, "The Pandemic Election," BelferCenter.org, April 2021, https://bit.ly/3jySqeQ.

like hell."[22] We will read interviews from US Capitol Police, specifically Black officers describing the racial slurs and threats that were directed toward them by the rioters during the siege.[23]

I want my students to use what they learned from Reconstruction to assume a position in the current debate over whether what happened on January 6 reflects who we are as a country—and where we might be going.

The Fight over CRT and the Rise of the New Lost Cause

I am fully aware that many teachers have found themselves in a precarious situation teaching a more comprehensive and inclusive narrative of this country, complete with the voices of both the heard and unheard, without being accused of teaching Critical Race Theory (CRT) by parents or administrators. The irony is that parents have been filling school board meetings across the country to express their opposition to CRT. But I have yet to see or hear one of these protesters accurately define or even describe what CRT is. The theory was first coined in the 1980s by Kimberlé Williams Crenshaw, a law professor at Columbia Law School and the University of California at Los Angles School of Law. Crenshaw described her thesis as:

> [A] way of seeing, attending to, accounting for, tracing and analyzing the ways that race is produced . . . the ways that racial inequality is facilitated, and the ways that our history has created these inequalities that now can be almost effortlessly reproduced unless we attend to the existence of these inequalities.[24]

22 "Trump Encourages Those At His Rally To March To The Capitol," *NBC News*, January 7, 2021, YouTube video, 1:03, https://bit.ly/3vjGCmu.

23 Allan Smith, "Black Police Officer Gives Emotional Account of Racial Attacks From Jan. 6 Mob," *NBC News*, July 27, 2021, https://nbcnews.to/3vdeFfV.

24 Jacey Fortin, "Critical Race Theory: A Brief History," *New York Times*, November 8, 2021, https://nyti.ms/3uyDFyY. There are a wide number of other definitions of CRT, including Time magazine (https://bit.ly/3GnqYtO) and Snopes (https://bit.ly/34n9S1E).

Professor Crenshaw outlined the components of CRT after trying to understand why racism persisted in society and her college campus after the triumphs of the 1950s and 1960s well into the 1980s.[25] Other academics, such as Professor Mari Matsuda of the William S. Richardson School of Law, described CRT as "a map for change." She argued:

> [CRT] is a method that takes the lived experience of racism seriously, using history and social reality to explain how racism operates in American law and culture, toward the end of eliminating the harmful effects of racism and bringing about a just and healthy world for all.[26]

Crenshaw had foreseen that in keeping with historical patterns in the United States, even a modest societal reform could "create tremendous backlash." The professor also knew that there was a risk that the backlash against CRT might be more lasting than the reform itself.[27] So it was perhaps not surprising to her that fear and misunderstandings dogged CRT. This is due in no small part to the sometimes breathtakingly dishonest ways that some political leaders and media outlets addressed it. For example, in a 2021 op-ed piece, former president Trump said that CRT was "designed to brainwash" students and was both "toxic and anti-American." He claimed that it advocated "judging people by the color of their skin [as] a good idea," and that it taught that the United States is "systemically evil."[28]

So, what about backlash for teachers accused of explicitly or implicitly teaching CRT or other "divisive" topics? Tennessee high school teacher Matt Hawn tried to discuss white privilege with respect to racially charged incidents, including Kyle Rittenhouse's fatal shootings of demonstrators in Wisconsin, the 2016 presidential

---

25 Ibid.

26 Ibid.

27 KK Ottesen, "An Architect of Critical Race Theory," *Washington Post*, January 22, 2022, https://wapo.st/3o9OAM0.

28 Donald J. Trump, "A Plan to Get Divisive & Radical Theories Out of Our Schools," *RealClearPolitics*, June 18, 2021, https://bit.ly/33sS5WW.

election, and the January 6 insurrection. Hawn was dismissed in 2021 after showing his students a performance by poet Kyla Jenée Lacey titled "White Privilege" for class discussion.[29] Hawn strongly believed that his own stance on racism and alleged support of CRT led to the school board's decision to terminate him.[30]

Dr. James Whitfield, then a principal at Colleyville Heritage High School in Texas, defended Hawn in a letter to the Texas school community. "Education is the key to stomping out ignorance, hate, and systemic racism," he offered, "a necessary conduit to get 'liberty and justice for all.'"[31] Dr. Whitfield was the first Black principal in his high school's history, and he received an overwhelmingly positive response from his majority white community. But a controversy ensued as he was accused by angry parents of promoting CRT.

A number of other administrators then resigned after being accused of teaching CRT or far left ideologies that were antithetical to Christian values. Many of them feared for their physical safety and mental well-being, despite having been assigned the responsibility in their respective districts of promoting school diversity addressing racism.[32] They included Rydell Harrison, a Black school superintendent in Redding, Connecticut; Brittany Hogan, the only Black administrator in Eureka, Missouri, and diversity coordinator in Missouri's Rockwood School District; and four administrators with the Carroll Independent School District in Southlake, Texas. These findings validate the fear many educators have about teaching sensitive issues with regard to race and US history.

Further, I strongly believe that the experiences of these educators will become more common. In 2021, the Brookings Institute published a survey of school districts and states that had

29 Emma Green, "He Taught a Ta-Nehisi Coates Essay. Then He Was Fired." *The Atlantic*, August 17, 2021, https://bit.ly/38AuTbe.

30 Ibid.

31 Brian Lopez, "How a Black High School Principal Was Swept Into a "Critical Race Theory" Maelstrom In a Mostly White Texas Suburb," *Texas Tribune*, September 13, 2021, https://bit.ly/3E54bDt.

32 Daniel Villarreal, "Death Threats and Fights over Critical Race Theory Have Driven at Least Six Educators to Resign," *Newsweek*, July 14, 2021, https://bit.ly/3JA4APn.

successfully banned or attempted to ban CRT in their classrooms.[33] The list has since grown to include Virginia, whose new governor banned CRT less than a month into his tenure and even instituted a "tip line" for parents to report any educator "behaving objectionably."[34] According to Dianne Carter de Mayo, a high school history teacher in Gloucester County, "someone's career and livelihood could be endangered" by the new Virginia law. "It's scaring people to death."[35]

Students today ask questions about CRT despite their parents' best efforts to shield them from the effects of systemic racism. According to a 2021 *USA Today*/Ipsos poll, about three out of four parents believe that schools should teach about slavery and racism as part of US history.[36] However, that "fourth" parent could take extreme stands against the perceived excesses and injustices of CRT. But in a way, the opinions of educators and parents might be moot. After all, the video of George Floyd's murder was broadcast into the homes of white, Black, Latin, Asian, suburban, urban, and upper-, middle-, and lower-class families around the world. Whether we as educators use CRT to help explain how and why this is still happening in a "post-racial" United States or not, our students want answers.

For the record, CRT is not a required subject in any K–12 public school in the United States. Per *PBS NewsHour*, "There is little to no evidence that Critical Race Theory itself is being taught to K–12 public school students, though some ideas central to it, such as lingering consequences of slavery, have been."[37]

Furthermore, CRT is not indoctrination. It is a graduate-level academic theory that has been woven into a straw man by certain

33 Rashawn Ray and Alexandra Gibbons, "Why Are States Banning Critical Race Theory?" *Brookings Institution*, November 2021, https://brook.gs/3JBgok8.

34 Sophia Ankel, "Virginia's New Republican Governor, Who Banned Critical Race Theory in Schools, Is Launching a Tip Line for Parents to Report Their Kids' Teachers," *Insider*, January 25, 2022, https://bit.ly/3E4bHyt.

35 Mel Leonor, "'It's Scaring People to Death': Youngkin's Tip Line Fuels Anger From the Left, Fear From Black Teachers," *Richmond Times-Dispatch*, January 29, 2022, https://bit.ly/3KzQ2R5.

36 Erin Richards and Alia Wong, "Parents Want Kids to Learn About Ongoing Effects of Slavery – but Not Critical Race Theory. They're the Same Thing." *USA Today*, September 20, 2021, https://bit.ly/3xhsEEa.

37 "Critical Race Theory is a Flashpoint for Conservatives, but What Does It Mean?" *PBS NewsHour*, November 4, 2021, https://to.pbs.org/3s5zFUh.

parties for their own purposes. Nevertheless, it is not inconceivable that you might find yourself accused of teaching CRT in the classroom when you are simply teaching social studies, and too many fine educators have already lost their jobs for doing just that—their jobs which do not require teaching CRT.

Students have the right to know the history of their country from the best-educated, certified, and experienced professionals in the subject. I believe teachers can safely teach tough historical events with effective scaffolding questions rooted in the analysis of primary sources. I will never offer my opinion when a student asks me what I think about a subject. Instead, I always reply, "What do the primary sources tell you?" I often use questions with the following stems:

1. How did X's experience differ from Y's?
2. To what extent was X's experience of a particular event shaped or influenced by A, and how do you know?
3. How did the laws at that time influence or shape X or Y's experience, and how do you know?
4. To what extent do communities today share that same experience, and why?

I also advise teachers to encourage students to reflect on their sources. For example, in the lesson where my students compare and contrast Thomas Nast's "Colored Rule in a Reconstructed (?) State" with Currier and Ives's 1872 lithograph, I would ask students to consider how these images can shape future generations' views of Reconstruction. I would also ask which depiction of Reconstruction most closely aligns with my students' understanding of the event.

Teachers might also consider asking the students the "reflections questions" I posed in my Voting Rights Act class. Ask your students:

1. How did what you learned challenge or reaffirm an existing belief or understanding you had?
2. What aspect of the lesson do you think everyone should be educated about?
3. How will what you learned impact how you see current events?

None of the above questions could reasonably be considered indoctrination for CRT or any other school of thought beyond what we call "critical thinking." Instead, the questions help teachers like me fulfill our roles as educators. They guide our students through history with effective questions rooted in primary sources. They allow students to come to their own conclusion and understanding of the world.

With regard to hot button issues, I firmly believe that this is the time for teachers to hold firm and draw a line in the sand. We cannot succumb to the same forces as McCarthyism wielded by politicians today to rally their base around a modernized Lost Cause. The situation is as dire today as it was during the Jim Crow era, when supporters of the Confederacy openly rewrote history by erecting monuments influencing school curricula and textbooks.

One such monument stood in front of Grant Parish Courthouse from 1951 until 2021.[38] It stated that on "this site occurred the Colfax Riot in which three white men and 150 Negroes were slain. This event on April 13, 1873, marked the end of carpetbag misrule in the South."[39] This marker was a topic of discussion with my students as they determined whether it accurately portrayed what happened in Colfax in 1873, how this marker alone influenced people's perception of the Colfax Massacre and Reconstruction, and how that marker reaffirmed or countered our classroom motto. Students are almost always able to identify the marker's hypocrisy and gross misrepresentation of events but end up wrestling with the fact that the marker is still there today.

Consider how politicians hid in the Capitol during the January 6 insurrection as rioters went from room to room, looking for Vice President Mike Pence and other leaders to confront and perhaps even to hang. Consider how many of those same hidden leaders later minimized what happened that day or even celebrated the event. Consider how the vast majority of US House and Senate

---

38 Tom Barber and Jeff Crawford, "Removing the White Supremacy Marker at Colfax, Louisiana: A 2021 Success Story," *The Journal of the Civil War Era*, July 6, 2021, https://bit.ly/3jzLb6B.

39 Lewis, "The 1873 Colfax Massacre Crippled the Reconstruction Era."

Republicans adamantly opposed a bipartisan commission to investigate the January 6 attack.[40] And a mere four months after the insurrection, Rep. Andrew Clyde (R-Ga.) referred to the rioters as "orderly," adding, "You know, if you didn't know the TV footage was a video from January the 6th, you would actually think it was a normal tourist visit."[41]

Calculated disinformation like this proves that future generations are at risk of being presented with a completely different version of the insurrection. It is also proof enough for me that if we do not teach history the way we have been trained to as educators, years from now there might be a marker erected on the US Capitol grounds declaring that the 2021 insurrectionists were "heroes."

Alysha Butler-Arnold is a veteran social studies teacher and author. She graduated from Florida Atlantic University with bachelor's and master's degrees in history. She was recognized as the 2019 History Teacher of the Year by the District of Columbia Daughters of the American Revolution, and the 2019 Gilder Lehrman National History Teacher of the Year for her innovative lessons and civic projects. In 2019, she was a DC Community Cornerstone awardee, and in 2020 became the first teacher ever appointed to the Gilder Lehrman Board of Trustees. She has presented at the National Conference for the Social Studies conference, Council of Chief State School Officers' Social Studies Collaborative, and Middle States Council for Social Studies.

40 Ryan Nobles, Ted Barrett, Manu Raju, and Alex Rogers, "Senate Republicans Block January 6 Commission," *CNN,* May 28, 2021, https://cnn.it/3juzPAT.

41 Chris Cillizza, "A Republican House Member Just Described January 6 As a 'Normal Tourist Visit,'" *CNN* online, May 13, 2021, https://cnn.it/3jsteH7.

CHAPTER 2

Responsiveness and Disruption: Be the Change Our Students Need

Nicole Butler-Hooton
Irving Elementary School, Oregon

Learning is a lifelong journey, which makes the time we spend at its beginning one of the most influential moments in our lives. A single lesson can change a person's outlook of the world and their understanding of humanity—themselves included. This places an enormous responsibility on social studies teachers as they guide students through history, including its past and present inequities and injustices.

In this chapter, Nicole Butler-Hooton shares how inclusion and cultural responsiveness can transform schools and their communities into the environments our students need. It is a method that Oregon Governor Kate Brown praised as "the power to shape our future for generations to come, … her seamless incorporation of equity into the classroom."

Dominator culture has tried to keep us all afraid, to make us choose safety instead of risk, sameness instead of diversity. Moving through that fear, finding out what connects us, revelling in our differences; this is the process that brings us closer, that gives us a world of shared values, of meaningful community.

– bell hooks[1]

Student Voice and Identity

When I first began my teaching career 16 years ago in a second-grade classroom, I vividly recall displaying a poster up on my wall that read: "Whose voice is missing and whose voice is included?" As a first-year teacher, I often referred to this poster to encourage students to think critically about learning, identity, and the institution of school and how our choices and beliefs can affect our individual identity and the identity of others.

This poster stayed with me throughout my career and each year I would use it in class discussions to create meaningful and reflective dialogue and discourse with students. The poster and the meaning behind it fit the needs of my classroom community. Students as young as second grade were able to find entry points into asking questions and beginning to think critically about voice and inclusion. The message of the poster was a metaphor for the work of hope and struggle we see inside the walls of our classrooms. But more importantly, the poster's words provided a bridge for identity and learning. It led students to a space where they could be their authentic self and access the truths and histories of other diverse people.

The community of learners need spaces in their K–12 classrooms to make sense of who they are and who they are not. Students of color in particular are flooded with images and representation in media, literature, and social media that depict their identities in deficit ways.[2] But trust is created through a rich

1 bell hooks, *Teaching Community: A Pedagogy of Hope* (New York: Routledge, 2003) 197.

2 Gholdy Muhammad, *Cultivating Genius: An Equity Framework for Culturally and Historically Responsive Literacy* (New York: Scholastic, 2020), 53–54.

environment that promotes social justice and encourages students to ask questions. The identity poster was a metaphor for social justice in my classroom at the beginning of my career. I really loved having the sign up in the classroom for students to reference when we were reading, engaging in math problems, and for overall developing of their racial consciousness.

Jean Moule in *Cultural Competence: A Primer for Educators*, says that when young students hear the stories of people of color (or POC), they tend to "deeply and sincerely share the feelings of the storyteller" and "connect with the lived experiences of others."[3] If this is happening in our classrooms today, then our stories become bridges of healing and strength. What stories are told in your classroom spaces?

Last year, a colleague who is now a college professor asked if I still had the "Whose voice is missing and whose voice is included?" poster in my classroom. She went on to explain how impactful that poster was to her when she visited my room as a practicum and program supervisor all those years ago—to her journey as an educator. My colleague wanted to use a similar concept to teach about equity principles, identity, and learning around reflective practice in her teacher education class. From our conversation, I heard how influential the sign had been in her personal equity journey. I, too, reflected, and still see the value in such questions being posed to our students as they engage in learning.

When I think back to the beginning of my career and how difficult it seemed to reach every student, I am reminded of the journey of teaching with a view that supports racial healing and culturally responsive pedagogies. To support racial healing, I always try to speak freely and openly about race and culture in my classroom, with my colleagues, and with parents. My hope, much like Moules's, is that students and colleagues will imitate such behavior "in their own conversations," learning, "and writings."[4] In becoming culturally competent, educators look to teach students

---

3 Jean Moule, *Cultural Competence: A Primer for Educators*, 2nd ed. (Belmont, CA: Wadsworth, 2012), 30.

4 Moule, *Cultural Competence*, 20.

to think critically about the world and social structures in which they exist.

Productive learning for students has to mean they will resist incorrect and harmful messages about themselves and others. One of the ways I support this work is to display books from diverse authors and bring in guest speakers who are people of color, as well as those engaged in social justice work, to represent authentic voices and cultural presence.

When we are learning about the Indigenous Peoples of Oregon, I look to the cultural resources of particular Nations and invite their cultural stewards to come into class. In the past we have engaged in drumming, salmon ceremonies, storytelling, and language development of multiple Indigenous Nations around the United States. These experiences produce learning that will help students thrive in our diverse world. In her book *Coaching for Equity*, Elena Aguilar states that we need to talk about race "in schools, in families, in our country, and in our world" to support a path of racial healing.[5] As we address sensitive topics in social studies in today's classroom, the need for racial healing calls on us to promote all children's healthy racial identity and awareness and to seek partnership with those voices who are marginalized. The community partnerships promote a collective feeling of healing within our schools and classrooms.

It is critical that we recognize each of our lived experiences and how they impact our teaching. I was born and raised on the rural Oregon coast, and my life has been a journey of self-discovery, influence, change, and power. As an Indigenous woman, growing up on the Oregon coast as one of the very few students of color in my town, school, and community presented an even bigger journey of access and equity. It has been a healing journey where I have had to position myself with intentionality in the educational system, making connections with my teachers and encouraging them to be co-learners in understanding more about my Indigenous culture.

---

5 Elena Aguilar, *Coaching for Equity: Conversations That Change Practice* (Hoboken, NJ: Jossey-Bass, 2020), 117.

As a young student, I was one of the only Brown and Indigenous students in my classroom, my town, and for many counties around. I did not see other students who looked like me nor did I see educators who resembled me. My identity was not accurately or positively depicted in textbooks, curriculum, and stories. The curriculum was not historically accurate or culturally relevant, and the Indigenous history I received was filled with negative stereotypes, violence, and trauma. In elementary school, I was not taught traditional stories and I did not see Indigenous examples of resilience and beauty.

The result of having very little culturally responsive teaching left me feeling unseen in the curriculum. The textbooks and picture books that had Indigenous People were mostly shown as people of the past and those whose culture had been erased. Because of these childhood experiences, I always had a desire to strengthen the Indigenous presence in my peer groups and in the community.

As a 40-year-old woman, educator, and leader, my equity journey is still emerging, growing, and rising. For me as a Native student, I desperately wanted to be accurately seen in books and for my culture to be valued for the beauty, power, and presence it stands for. The reminder that American history is Native history is a concept I use to guide my practice, and I will discuss development of Native curricular units later in the chapter. Diversifying curriculum can start with building a sustainable classroom library of culturally relevant books. But Gholdy Muhammad reminds us the mere addition of multicultural books does not mean the curriculum is culturally and historically responsive, as access and representation alone does not translate into full equity.[6]

Using diverse books and having conversations that support power and presence must become part of an educator's core values. When selecting books for students, please consider these questions: Do the books in my classroom represent diverse cultures in both the text and the images? Do the textbooks and curriculum materials reflect multiple points of view? Are diverse names, people, culture groups, and objects represented in stories, examples, and academic content?

6 Muhammad, *Cultivating Genius*, 54.

For the next part of this section, please reflect on what parts of your identity have allowed you more privilege. Further, think about accurate representations in the literature, assignments, and materials used in your classroom space, and how this can allow students to feel seen. I often think about the connection between my identity and the knowledge I now have after 16 years in the classroom as an educator. What parts of your identity do you show and celebrate, and what parts of your identity do you leave behind as you enter educational systems? How do we "know" the texts and materials we are using are purposeful, authentic, and embrace identity?

The proximity to whiteness and the experiences of my family's indoctrinated, prescribed feelings of inadequacy and racial discrimination was something I noted and lived throughout my K–12 experience. There were countless racist acts my family experienced, and I saw and lived these microaggressions and unfair stereotypes placed on my family.

The historical trauma I stepped into is still happening in our classrooms today through dated, inaccurate classroom materials and bias within the educator mindset. These can include stereotypes that encourage a narrative that perpetuates inequalities. School structures and systems are ingrained with settler colonialism mindsets. As Native People and Native students, we need to see and hear more Native stories. There is a desire for "our people" to move past the Native invisibility. These same feelings can be seen and felt within other marginalized communities.

When I consider the healing, centering relationships, and support students of color deserve, it begins with the disruption of systems that don't serve all students. To engage in Indigenous history and lifeways, there needs to be a shift from an academic mindset to a human-centered approach to learning. Shifts are beautiful when we think about initiating the repair. And approaches centered in learning and understanding the histories and identities of our students can be implemented for the future of our educational systems.[7]

7 Muhammad, *Cultivating Genius*, 45.

We've all heard the quote attributed to Gandhi: "Be the change you wish to see in the world." And for me, when students, parents, and community members say they have felt seen in my space, curriculum, and in my presence, that feeling is the change. The divine feeling of a student connecting to education and feeling empowered in our schools is my goal for teaching. The sense of belonging and empowerment from our students, families, and communities builds a bridge to human-centered approaches to teaching.

When educators lean in and listen to students, we will see the learning become more meaningful and the empowerment of our students will shine through. This work can be hard and uncomfortable at times. Teachers are often seeking to expand their students' ability to do a certain task or learn a particular topic. I always say if you're not sitting in discomfort as you do the equity work, then you probably are not doing this work in a meaningful way.

Students are in desperate need of human-centered approaches to learning. But the question remains, how do we get there?

If we can use our students to guide our curricular choices, we become the change-makers, the disruptors, the lifelong learners. Ask your students about their culture! Start with a culture unit and get to know the students who are occupying space in your classrooms. Next, engage with the ethnic or racial identity of your students to build your classroom culture. Other ideas include finding foods and languages that define the student's culture. We have such rich discussions over foods that are part of each student's family life. Visualizing a kitchen table where all your students have a seat is a great metaphor for equity and inclusive practice. It can be impactful to discuss traditions, keepsakes, routines, and family structures with your students. In doing so, you're able to create so much space for representation. And that representation matters! The impact will be felt if you ask your student, "Who is one teacher who has changed your life or who is one teacher who made you feel special today?"

Educators who take risks and allow for meaningful conversations even at the expense of feeling discomfort are the Real Ones.

Power and Privilege

When teaching about history and race, teachers have to do the heavy lift to educate themselves and find entry points into teaching about multiple perspectives. By diving into such resources, we are sometimes more open to accepting our privilege and power and how power can relate to marginalization. Through strong relationships, consistent communication, and listening, educators can uncover the stories of their students and families and use them to guide the learning and curriculum. We must honor the stories, experiences, and emotions of our students to build stronger communities. How are you connecting with families in meaningful ways?

In my graduate course, I was introduced to a Privilege Walk activity and then was able to reflect on my level of privilege, generalize my discoveries to a learning environment, and consider how diversity and privilege might influence educational settings. First steps of impact include authentic relationships and sense of self, a realization of the power our students hold, and regard for honesty and access to a more truthful education. Remind yourself to realize the difference of intent versus impact. Next, the internal privilege work allows for the question of how we set and support students for success when access is something students from marginalized populations are always struggling with, especially our Black and Brown students. Consider the extent of the work and know that you do not have to be an expert. Equity work can be lonely but can also create allies and build and grow your networking opportunities.

Reflection Question: How has historical or generational trauma affected your role in your classroom or system?

How do I teach about culture, race, and equity in the classroom? I start with a reminder that we cannot teach about these topics until we can do it "correctly." When I say correctly, I am referring to recognizing that the ability to do what is necessary to meet the needs of culturally different students may be limited by the rules and atmosphere of the school. Are you adapting to the cultural needs of your students, and do you have supportive efforts of the larger system to supply culturally competent education?[8]

This work can feel hard, uncomfortable, and uncertain but we are bound to do this work with correct information and knowledge so we feel prepared to share authentic, accurate, perspectives. This resonates with me because I know that to do the critical work about racial healing and policy change in education, conversations about race and inequity must be happening.

When starting a unit on Black Indigenous People of Color (BIPOC), the work can begin with asking students what they think of when they hear the words "Indian," "Native American," or "African American," for example. I then make a list of all the things students generate so that I can begin to discover gaps and learning needs. Upon making the list of words and images students dictate, I commonly notice misconceptions, generalizations, or harmful stereotypes. From this information, I can begin to find entry points into disrupting oppressive history. How are you beginning the unit of diverse groups of people and how often are you teaching about and disrupting harmful stereotypes in your space?

Cultural Knowledge

I was recently in an affinity group space with educators of color, and I heard someone mention that inequity must be witnessed to be changed. I had to sit with this comment and allow for growth and more understanding. What kind of inequities allow for practitioners to be more reflective? When the basic needs of our families and students in our classrooms are not being met, teaching and learning become barriers and create conflict in cultural knowledge. Oftentimes, we must sit with discomfort, educate ourselves, and find entry to move forward in this equity work. Furthermore, when research "consistently shows that schools are not always welcoming places for culturally diverse students," such problems are too widespread to be ignored.[9] Finding approaches to grasp the social

8 Moule, *Cultural Competence*, 17.
9 Moule, *Cultural Competence*, 5.

reality of race and identity in the United States can allow educators to be more human-centered in their understanding of teaching and learning.

Our students and communities deserve to learn accurate history and they benefit from multiple historical perspectives. We must be intentional and reflective when we teach sensitive topics or racialized topics. I am passionate about teaching topics such as the First Americans, Indigenous People, tribal names and history, restoration of Indigenous tribes, influential Black Americans, segregation, intersectionality, stereotypes of Asian Americans, Native American boarding schools, and both Black Joy and Black Lives Matter.

As I am not an expert on any of the aforementioned topics so when preparing to teach, I have to use a critical viewpoint and have a layered approach to develop and build strong units so students feel connected to the new learning. I address my biases, gaps in learning, and build relationships with members of the communities. Space needs to be created for our students to ask questions and engage in the new learning in authentic ways. When teaching about diverse groups, I remind myself of this quote by Derald Wing Sue: "As long as microaggressions remain hidden, invisible, unspoken, and excused as innocent slights with minimal harm, we will continue to insult, demean, alienate, and oppress marginalized groups."[10]

In my Native unit studies, I teach about land acknowledgment as an entry point. By acknowledging the land we reside on, and which Nation this land belonged to, ensures students—both Native and non-Native—are learning about cultural experiences different from their own and are cultivating a relationship with land and a deeper understanding of Indigenous culture.

I reside on the traditional homelands of the Kalapuya Tribe of Oregon. Following the Willamette Valley Treaty of 1855, these people were forcibly removed and are now descendants of the Confederated Tribes of Siletz of Oregon and Confederated Tribes of

---

10 Derald Wing Sue and Lisa Beth Spanierman, *Microaggressions in Everyday Life*, 2nd ed. (Hoboken, NJ: John Wiley & Sons, 2020), 29.

Grand Ronde of Oregon. When delivering a land acknowledgment I also address that many Native lands are still being occupied due to deceptive and broken treaties. My goal is to first bring in an authentic voice or community members who are experts in the field I'm teaching on. There are signs and posters up in my room that say, "You are on Indigenous Land" and "You are on the Indigenous Homelands of the Kalapuya Tribe." I will invite a local tribal member in to give a land acknowledgment. In the past, we have had opportunities to visit nearby cultural museums and the University of Oregon Longhouse.

Gholdy Muhammed concluded that "cultural relevance is equity-centered and charges educators to engage in practices that push for social justice."[11] Social justice in today's classrooms can look and feel quite different for each of us. What does social justice look like for you in your lessons and units? How do you honor the Native People who came before you and how do you recognize the land on which you live?

Disruption

I have been asked countless times about how to address barriers to policy and practice in our schools. My first response is to unapologetically disrupt systems that don't serve all students.

How do you speak up and change practices to allow students to "get factual and meaningful information" and "understand the histories of oppressed groups"?[12] I am a proponent of having conversations that change practice and focus on culturally responsive lessons to expand my own "equity lens." This is my pathway to think critically about how to promote inclusion, diversity, and emotional learning as a catalyst to disrupt systems that don't serve all students or people.Educators can develop their own equity lens through creating an equity stance that includes, "I am," "I believe," and "I will" statements to guide their reason and beliefs for teaching. These can act as a way for us to align

---

11 Muhammed, *Cultivating Genius*, 45.

12 Moule, *Cultural Competence*, 25.

our initiatives. The equity lens and stance are frameworks that require educators to shift to valuing and building on the cultures, languages, strengths and opportunities that every child brings to their educational experience.

For educators, this can include calling out a colleague to address an unjust act you may have witnessed, rethinking material that seems racially insensitive or inaccurate, or avoiding materials that are not representative of the community you're teaching about or within.

I have had to disrupt systems I've navigated in for 40 years as a woman of color and as a Citizen of the Confederated Tribes of Siletz Indians and San Carlos Apache Tribe. I have become a disruptor of a colonized mindset and an educator who understands I have privilege. I think critically about whose voice is being highlighted, celebrated, and engaged, and whose voice is missing. My privilege allows me to be a voice for my communities and those whose voice is not represented in curriculum and systems.

Getting to know my students with a culture unit has allowed me to see my students and their backgrounds in a true fashion. I can get to know my families and encourage my students to bring in their culture and family values into the classroom. By acknowledging each learner's cognitive, linguistic, social, and emotional development influences on learning, I am more able to align my instructional decisions that build on the students' strengths and needs. Language is instrumental in healing the needs of communities and my goal is to try and incorporate mini-lessons based on the cultural needs of my students. I also use tribal language websites, Native speakers, and videos as resources.

As mentioned earlier, I am passionate about teaching Indigenous units about the nine federally recognized tribes in Oregon. In my second-grade classroom, I use our state's Tribal/Shared History curriculum as well as tribal curriculum. Each of the Nine Tribes in Oregon is developing place-based tribal curricula that have been vetted and will be available to support the state curriculum. These lessons connect to community organizations, such as theater groups at local universities, music programs, culture bearers or culture liaisons from communities of color, and through literature written by people of color.

Implementing Tribal/Shared History curriculum as well as seeking curriculum from Indigenous Nations creates a path of racial healing, innovative learning, and finding ways to be authentically curious.

In times of triumph, challenge, and perseverance, I become curious, accept the discomfort and begin to create new learning pathways for the journey to being an inspirational teacher who never stops learning. As an Indigenous teacher, I don't claim to know everything about my tribe or others, so I'm always wanting to gain more information and make more connections in the community. This learning is reflected on my bookshelves and book orders, with each of them growing every month. These books become resources for the teacher I strive to be.

When you feel that a lesson, novel, or mindset is not supporting our marginalized communities, how do you disrupt? What commitments do you make for further growth to support your relationships with your students?

Collaborative Inquiry

Collaborative inquiry allows the teacher and student to create authentic partnerships, and also helps teachers to feel supported within their buildings. Collaboration with families and within schools consists of reaching out in meaningful ways through dialogue at school, emails, newsletters, phone calls, and relationship building to understand family dynamics and living structures. Acknowledging equity, inclusion, school environment, and professional learning are the shared vision of collaborative inquiry. Addressing individual needs of families can also be a way to connect the lifeways of a community to educational spaces.

When I was a young child, my family experienced prominent levels of trauma and dysfunction but my teachers still made me feel seen and valued. Inevitably, these shifts transferred to educational and academic growth. Authentic partnerships are propelled by shifts of educator mindset to improve educational practices that supply opportunities for all students to be successful. Reflect on the ways you evaluate if your students' needs are being met. How do you collect empathy data?

For me, I've come to realize the teacher journey is about steps I've taken to be culturally proficient in engaging with others whose backgrounds and lived experience may be different from my own. When I started as a first-year teacher, and one who was still discovering what it meant to be Indian myself, this understanding of how to create rapport in the classroom was the first support I focused on. Building authentic relationships with students and families has allowed this work to happen seamlessly.

I often get asked to explain how I create environments in my room of connectedness, resilience, compassion, and rigor. These key concepts have led me toward an understanding that all students have a story that deserves to be told and acknowledged. It has everything to do with my connection and trust-building around opportunities for my students to tell their story and for me to be a part of their own cultural awareness. Meeting students where they are at in a particular time and stage allows us as educators to receive everyone freely.

Learning to Understand

I am a learner at heart and will always want to know more about the world and the racial climate I navigate in, which includes reexamining the world through different lenses.

In *Culturally Sustaining Pedagogies*, Django Paris boldly questions what pedagogies would look like in the United States if they were not dominated by what Toni Morrison described as "the White gaze."[13] How can we help students see themselves in curricula, textbooks, dialogue and discourse, disruptions of inequities? We cannot be afraid to show our responsiveness, our engagement, and our willingness to be innovative and find ways

---

13 Django Paris, *Culturally Sustaining Pedagogies: Teaching and Learning for Justice in a Changing World* (New York: Teachers College Press, 2017), 2–3.

to expand our learning. Our students notice when we take on this powerful role. To be an innovative teacher, please ask yourself: "What do I do to consider the perspectives and lived experience of my students?"

The thought I have each year as I begin to teach about "controversial" themes and lessons is how the humanization of lessons can allow for transformational change. This change may lead to a feeling of discomfort as we humanize our curriculum. It is also a sign of growing a cultural competence that respects and support learners' cultural characteristics, academic strengths and challenges, and social interactions.

A few years ago, as I was preparing to teach about the Black Lives Matter movement, I had to engage in reflective practice and find resources that were reliable. I felt so much growth happening and was able to create meaningful connections to my second graders as I used resources like the Zinn Education Project, the National Education Association EdJustice website, the Unsettling America decolonization site, and authentic voices from the Black community. This work has continued as I develop future units.

To think about diversifying practice, I honor the space I'm working through in regard to diversity practices, such as awareness of self, learning environment, understanding the learner, and professional practice. What units have you developed or used that may need more reflective practice to create restorative justice or racial equity?

In my experience, culturally responsive lessons are more aligned and accepted when students and families feel supported because relationships have been cultivated, nurtured, and maintained. This is not to say that I don't have parents who ask tough questions and ask to see materials being presented. However, the majority of lessons I have taught have allowed families entry points into an understanding that learning is a basic human need. Proper communication from the teacher can realize the "purpose of education" envisioned by Aguilar:

...to provide students with skills and knowledge so that they become critical thinkers, compassionate leaders, and self-actualized people who contribute to the healing and transformation of this world.[14]

Barriers

Education in the United States did not start with Black and Brown people in mind. I have had this conversation with staff and administrators alike. I try to come from a lived experience story and then a historical trauma perspective, and finally end these discussions with the future of education and how we can create a new educational legacy for all students.

Recently, I had the opportunity to listen to Secretary of Education Miguel Cardona remind us that the time is right to reimagine educational spaces. I then spent time wondering and dreaming about educational possibilities for sustainable ways to impact change. Acknowledging that there is work to be done only solidifies the personal struggles we all face in education daily and thus has encouraged me to believe in the power and intention of education.

In school, I was a struggling Title 1 student who couldn't read in first grade. I had a Speech Individualized Education Plan, received language services, and grappled with so many negative mindsets about my culture. Yet I had educators who looked to me for the unique gifts and talents I did possess. There were so many barriers for me as a young child that have offered me space to reflect on these practices by asking, what is the purpose of schooling?

Experiences like these changed me, and I am now a firm believer in creating schools where all students feel like they belong and can see the value of education.

---

14 Aguilar, *Coaching for Equity*, 29.

Education of Love and Joy

Author and educator Bettina Love encourages us to build schools we thought were impossible to imagine: "Schools built on justice, love, joy, and anti-racism."[15]

As an Indigenous woman, you may begin to understand my lens, and I'm overcoming my own historical trauma of operating in a school system. Our students are aware of race and unfair treatment whether we talk about it or not. My lens is that we address racism and behaviors that perpetuate it, so we don't repeat the past. When a second grader says, "Mrs. Butler, why did that girl (Ruby Bridges) get treated so badly?", I think about how my students get to receive the truth and assumptions. When students feel safe to ask questions and wonder about racial equity, I ponder the answer and then attempt to reply in meaningful, accurate, and truthful ways that encourage students to have a voice and an understanding that their voice matters. This idea of shared power is sacred in educational spaces. How do you share power in your class and space?

When I hear students in celebration and agreement that they love learning about Native Americans, or influential African Americans, or want to challenge ideologies that don't serve all people, I have initiated some repair of racial healing. These revelations are supplying the essential understandings of the context of social studies in education and reparations.

When students ask the anti-oppressive questions that I get every year surrounding racial equity, racism, structures, and systems that perpetuate inequalities, what should teachers do? I have witnessed teachers interrupting patterns of discrimination through accurate, shared history, dialogue, and effective questioning. But I have also seen many educators shy away from controversial or sensitive topics. These are the uncomfortable questions that make teachers think, "Wow, did they really ask that?" Yet those are the questions that need responses to propel the work forward.

---

15 Bettina L. Love, *"Dear White Teachers: You Can't Love Your Black Students If You Don't Know Them,"* Education Week, March 18, 2019, https://bit.ly/3E8ft9T.

How we disrupt and insert ourselves into implementation of culturally relevant information is the "why" for our work. How we "move the dial" comes is the next part. For me, strengthening the Indigenous presence in today's classrooms and systems is my heart's work. I can continue to teach about Native People through power and presence and by bringing my own culture to the classroom. I show pictures of my grandparents who were forcibly removed to attend boarding school, stripped of their culture and forced to assimilate. I also share stories of my own journey as a Native woman, mother, teacher, and leader. Students are very honest and will say very unapologetically that they didn't know Indian people still lived today.

When we look at honoring our Native students and families, we are decolonizing education and reflecting on ways to repair relationships. Indigenizing educational spaces is a way to extend the respect and healing to Tribal People. The strengths, assets, and contributions our Native American students bring to their communities is a mindset we must adopt. Let's be reminded that many students don't feel seen in the curriculum, nor do they feel lessons accurately depict their culture. Take a minute and reflect. Was there ever a part of your identity you had to hide?

To end this chapter, I'd like to remind us to think back to the needs of the group you are teaching while considering sustainable practices, conversations, cultural norms, and how you can connect the standard to learning and still maintain multiple perspectives. It's a lot to consider. But we can all reflect back on our own educational journey and consider what was absent from our history lessons. Let us use those deficits to project our equity work and growth. We must remind ourselves to critically analyze whose needs are being centered for healing, so that students can reflect and have an opportunity to speak.

Teaching is a daily struggle for social justice. By promoting equity and challenging frameworks that do not serve all students, we help young people "develop the agency to build a better world."[16]

---

16 Muhammad, *Cultivating Genius*, 12.

Honoring our spaces of learning and humanizing our classrooms means educators are focused on unity and the commitment to support all students, families, and communities. The journey to be culturally responsive educators is social justice work. It is rooted in identity and community education.

Educate yourself enough
So that you may understand
The ways of the other people
But not too much
That you may lose
Your understanding
Of your own

–Lemalu Tate Simi "Identity" (1995)[17]

Nicole Butler-Hooton, 2021 Oregon Teacher of the Year, was a second-grade teacher at Irving Elementary School in Eugene, Oregon for 15 years. She has now taken on the role of mentor coach/instructional teacher on special assignment in the Bethel School District, mentoring and coaching new teachers. She is also Eugene/Springfield's local representative for the Oregon Indian Educator Association. Butler-Hooton is a Siletz and Apache tribal member committed to the values of family, student voice, community, and growth, both within and outside her classroom. She believes that Indigenous children need access to a more truthful education that allows them to realize their Indigenous self-identity, language, and culture through accurate representation in their lives.

---

17 *Indigenous and Decolonizing Studies in Education: Mapping the Long View*, eds. Linda Tuhiwai Smith, Eve Tuck, and K. Wayne Yang (New York: Routledge, 2019), 189.

CHAPTER 3

Word Is Bond: Stayin' Dope on Roads Untraveled

Gerardo Muñoz
Denver Center for International Studies, Colorado

Social studies teachers often walk a tightrope, balancing community expectations and statewide requirements against an honest portrayal of history and current events. Gerardo Muñoz is a master of this art, and the following essay revisits times he encountered, confronted, and learned from similar challenges throughout his two decades in education. He also shares a unique social studies project where his students introduced a topic that deepened their understanding of history through independent research of historical figures, marginalized groups, and understudied subjects.

Blowback and the BoogieDown

A few weeks ago, a fellow classmate in one of my doctoral classes asked me a question that caught me unawares: "How do you deal with pushback from administrators, parents, or students who may not agree with you?"

I had to reflect on this for a moment. To the surprise of many, particularly those who listen to my podcasts or follow me on social media, I could not recall a time when any members of my school community resisted or disputed my teaching in any meaningful way. In turn, I realized that I don't have a common or predictable way to address the challenges facing history and social studies teachers today.

So let me state upfront that I do not possess a prescriptive method or framework that will win you friends and respect from your students. Instead, I have learned to embrace what I will call an "untraveled road" in my teaching, because it centers on students' ideas and identities.

In this piece, I will explain the humanizing method that I propose. There will be gems and practices that you may find beneficial in the following pages. And while these stories and strategies might seem disconnected and even random, they are united by a path carved without a map, guided by students and their communities.

To return to my classmate's question above, let me explain why there was only a small likelihood that I would experience the kind of political blowback that many of my teaching colleagues encountered across the country. I teach at an international studies school centered on global awareness, cultural competence, and world languages (we offered seven languages at the time). Our community has tended to be progressive, liberal-minded, and open to new ideas even when disillusioned by "traditional" politics.

On November 4, 2008, our school held a mock election for president of the United States, and then-Senator Barack Obama won by a substantial margin. When President-elect Obama was inaugurated two months later, my school attended the ceremony virtually. Even though I was an unknown teacher who had been in the community less than a year, I did not hide my beliefs or that I have always taught primarily Black and Brown students.

My classroom at the time was an argumentative space by design. I named it "the BoogieDown" in honor of hip-hop's birthplace and to continue the legacy of my former colleague, Shawne. The classroom itself seemed to have opinions, as students were greeted by an iconic poster of Malcolm X as they entered. The Black political activist was smiling, his left hand behind his head, and gazing up at who I imagine was a person speaking to him. A quotation below the poster read: "Of all our studies, history is best qualified to reward our research."[1]

I love this quote, and I have it emblazoned on every history syllabus I've created, including the ethnic studies classes I introduced to my school and AP World History. I want students to know that history is not a subject to bore them. It is not, as is sometimes thought, a list of agreed-on names, dates, and events that students must simply memorize in order to regurgitate for an exam. No, history is much more—it is what's happening *now*.

In fact, I believe the teaching of history as a reproduction of facts and interpretations looms as a reason that we have arrived at the present cultural crossroads. Teachers know that critical thinking and civic engagement have deteriorated significantly in recent years, and that process has been further eroded by the COVID-19 pandemic and the racist killings of Black men, women, and trans people.[2] The pandemic quarantine across the nation siloed us all, and no matter how many Zoom dinners, happy hours, or class meetings we shared, we did not have anyone to talk to, learn from, or connect with the way we used to. The pandemic dominated all thoughts and conversations.

---

1 Malcolm X, "Message to the Grass Roots," December 10, 1963, in *Malcolm X Speaks*, ed. George Breitman (New York: Grover Press, 1990), 8.

2 Rebecca Winthrop, "The Need for Civic Education in 21st-Century Schools," *Brookings Institution*, June 4, 2020, https://brook.gs/3KG30wE; Alan D. Blotcky, "Critical Thinking, COVID-19 Vaccines, and Deadly Consequences," *Psychiatric Times*, October 23, 2021, https://bit.ly/3vdgoSn; U.S. Government Accountability Office, K–12 Education: *Students' Experiences with Bullying, Hate Speech, Hate Crimes, and Victimization in Schools*, GAO-22-104341 (Washington, DC, 2021), 3, https://bit.ly/3JF09mi.

While we social studies teachers are hardly immune from this type of alienation, we pride ourselves on providing context that helps students make sense of these very trying times. Thus, we faced the added challenge of teaching history while braving some of the worst of it in modern memory.

Back to my classroom: Among its other wall decorations in the 2008–2009 school year was a red-and-black poster of Ernesto "Che" Guevara, who is another lightning-rod historical figure in today's culture wars. As an educator, I have always kept Guevara close to me. The more I study him, the more I find him to have been a layered and complex, imperfect person. Che figured prominently in my classroom as a reminder that injustice must be faced, no matter the inconvenience to those not personally experiencing the injustice. Furthermore, he is an important figure, especially for the two-thirds of my students who identify as Latinx.

I am reminded of a back-to-school night that same year. The father of one of my sixth graders raised his hand after my spiel and asked, "How do you use the revolutionary ideas of Malcolm X and Che Guevara to inform a pedagogy of liberation with your students?"

I gave a very stumbling answer, mindful of the nice white parents in the room, about the struggle for human rights, acceptance, and the willingness to change course when we learned new ideas. The parents seemed okay with the response. Also, without sounding immodest, most of their children adored me, so many issues may have been filtered through that lens.

Inaugural Turbulence

What follows here is a contentious, sensitive, real-time moment from my early days teaching social studies. As I stated earlier, we had an all-school assembly to watch the 2009 inauguration of Obama as the 44th president of the United States of America. Our assistant principal hooked up a speaker system to his laptop, connected the LCD projector, and rolled down the giant screen in the auditorium. Our principal and founder of the school took the stage in front of us, speaking about the triumph of democracy and the historical significance of the first Black president of the United States.

Then the feed began.

It was a truly beautiful and mesmerizing moment. Speeches were given, and the group of students in the auditorium, ranging from seventh to 12th grade, were completely silent, hanging on every word, savoring the historic moment. But then the ante was upped. When the audience in Washington, DC, was asked to rise, nearly every single person in the school auditorium stood. In an instant, it felt like we were in person, and to this day it is the closest I have ever come to attending such a historical event.

After the assembly, we returned to my classroom. I had a group of about 30 sixth graders, and I asked them to write about the historic moment they had just witnessed. Student after student read accounts about how inspired they felt and how exciting the inauguration was to watch, but one student was visibly frustrated. When it was his turn to speak, he said: "I don't know why everyone is so happy. Obama stole the election. He isn't even from America!"

His classmates became very upset, and an argument ensued.

I was not yet the 23-year veteran social studies teacher I am today, so I found the contentiousness alarming. I became terrified of what may happen next. When was the angry email coming? The conference? Or even a lawsuit? I remembered what happened to Jay Bennish, a social studies teacher from a neighboring district. His career has been dogged for the better part of two decades by his criticisms of the Bush administration, the wars in Iraq and Afghanistan, and the War on Drugs.[3] Did I have the wherewithal to stand up to the type of rage that seemingly could be passed on from parent to child?

At that stage in my career, I was still extremely fearful. I had heard stories of teachers who were railroaded for even hinting at their political beliefs. Controversial issues are literally written into our job descriptions, but how are we meant to address them?

---

3 Grant Stringer, "Cherry Creek Schools Drops Racism Allegations Against Lauded Overland Teacher Jay Bennish," *Sentinel Colorado*, July 24, 2020, https://bit.ly/3uw1veS.

I am sorry to report that I feel I had even turned my back on my own embattled colleagues, not wanting my career to end before it started. In short, I was not the outspoken teacher-leader that people see today. But I had colleagues who were outspoken, and they were fellow educators of color at that. I felt anxiety when these colleagues pushed back against the administration or parents. My chest tightened, my stomach turned, my hands shook when they spoke, because I knew that I should offer support. As the Peruvian philosopher José Carlos Mariátegui once wrote, "we are still too few to be divided."[4]

Yet I allowed myself to be alienated from my community, wanting only to survive. A barrage of images hit me when I thought of being an activist who might get fired: the five years I spent in college, the struggle in getting by, the ordeal of surviving on about one full meal per day. The memory of those hardships made me determined to stay employed, no matter the cost to myself.

All of which brings me back to the student who maintained that the newly inaugurated Obama was a noncitizen who had stolen the presidential election. I began to physically shake, and I asked the student, "Where did you hear that?"

He replied, "My parents followed the election, and Obama's definitely not from here."

I invited the student to come back the next day and share his sources. This was much to the chagrin of his classmates; many of them were children of color for whom this moment in history would be immortalized. Obama's inauguration was and would remain an essential part of their childhood.

Please don't get my reaction to the moment twisted. I am not a technician, trained and programmed to give certain responses in the classroom. I had a visceral reaction to the student's comments. The "birther" movement, as it would be called, had roots in the racist "othering" of people of color. Even progressives in my circle openly wondered if a man named Barack Hussein Obama could ever be elected president.

---

4 Harry E. Vanden and Marc Becker, eds., *José Carlos Mariátegui: An Anthology* (New York: Monthly Review Press, 2011), 342.

There were so many ways I could have chosen to reply. I could have retreated into my default state, which is to be accommodating and accepting. My tendency to avoid conflict, even if it's necessary. I could have responded through a frame of false equivalency, giving the saccharin response of "You see, children? We all have different opinions, and that is great!" But such a response would have made it acceptable to give time to unsubstantiated declarations, and would have created confusion for my 11- and 12-year-old middle schoolers as to what constitutes evidence in social discourse.

I also could have chosen to shame the student, shutting down his racist discourse by saying something like, "That's not true at all" or worse. Let me qualify my use of the word "racist" by saying that racism is not a personality type. Racism is not a character flaw. Racism is a system that is sustained by our collective actions. It is the information that US citizens have propagated that upholds racist systems. In this case, it is a system that casts people of color, immigrants, and members of minority and marginalized communities as "others" who do not have participatory rights in our political system.

Shutting down the "dissenting" student mentioned earlier may have been a correct response to the situation. Some of my friends and colleagues would not have hesitated to take that bold of a position. But I am also a deeply empathetic person, and I could remember times in my own intellectual past that I made uninformed declarations. I made these because I wanted to be seen. I wanted attention, which is an absolutely normal adolescent need.

I remember how I felt when I was called out for one of my zingers. I was in high school, and during a discussion of militarism, I declared, "Yo, the military is the only institution that can actually say mission accomplished." I sat back, waiting for my peers to concede defeat to my hot take.

That isn't what happened. Instead, one of my younger friends pushed back fiercely, asking, "And what is that mission? Death? Murder of innocents?"

My face went flush, and I felt like I was being stared at, judged by everyone. I do not remember how I escaped that conversation with our friendship intact. I have no recollection of what I said in response. But I didn't like how I felt. I learned from being challenged, but there is a key difference between this experience and the one I describe as a teacher. In the former, our power was more or less equal. In the latter, I had considerable power over a 12-year-old in a class I was teaching. That power dynamic has to be first and foremost in my thoughts.

I also realized that everything I had been taught about good teaching had broken down. I was taught that tight classroom management and good teaching eliminated any tension, discomfort, or potential conflict. I was taught to avoid controversial issues at all costs, because it potentially harmed students' optimism and resolve to do their assignments and learn the course content. I learned to examine my classroom not as a space separate from global political realities, but as a space contextualized by those realities. The notion that a classroom only provides reprieve from the troubles of the world is naive and harmful. Henry Giroux, the eminent scholar, once argued that the teacher ought to function as a public intellectual who allows students to address difficult and contentious issues in the classroom space.[5] And it was Dr. LaGarrett King of the University of Missouri's Carter Center for Black History who wrote that history should not be "manufactured into safe, sanitized and pleasant narratives," but taught honestly.[6]

These principles have become my ethos. As my friend Darren Kawaii, a brilliant principal in the Bay Area, once told me, "The absence of conflict does not equal peace."

In retrospect, a better response to the student who balked at Obama's inauguration may have been along the lines of "Thank you for sharing, [student name], but let's pause a second to give others a chance to respond." Others probably would have, but if they hadn't, I could have then posed an inquiry, for example, "I've heard this stated during this campaign, and I wonder where it comes from?"

5 Henry A. Giroux, *Teachers as Intellectuals: Toward a Critical Pedagogy of Learning* (Westport: Bergin & Garvey, 1988).

6 LaGarrett King, "Why Our Schools Aren't Doing Justice to the Complexities of Black History," *DesertNews*, June 17, 2021, https://bit.ly/3M2yMo2.

I could have even said, "So, I hear you, and I have heard this previously. It is my understanding that this theory has been disproven, but I could be wrong about that. Where might I be able to challenge my own understanding?" This could ostensibly model what a critical learner does: speak, by all means, speak. Because civility often cloaks hostility and advantages those already viewed as civil, i.e., those with power or privilege. But the critical learning praxis also includes maintaining intellectual honesty. Nobody knows everything. There is always new information available, and if it's valid, some of this information may cause us to shift our beliefs.

So while I view the "dissenting student" incident as a turning point for my practice, I may have missed an opportunity for transformative learning for all the students in the room. The students went about their normal business after the interaction. But as a teacher, I had mistaken control for comfort. I didn't want the trouble of managing or trying to control a group of highly charged and upset 11- and 12-year-olds. It was not a part of the lesson plan.

During student worktime, I wrote a short note and put it on the dissenting student's desk. I told him to never silence himself and to always be willing to share what he had learned. His father eventually emailed me. He thanked me for being supportive of his son, who had affixed the note to the mirror in his bathroom.

I don't think I would have handled the issue the same way today. For one thing, today's youth are much more connected to the 24-hour news cycle. That dissenting student would have been promptly "dragged" for pushing a position that (at best) is not supported by evidence, and at worst, was a lowly racial attack and an attempt to "other" another person. But I have learned over the years to pause and invite others to speak. And it all started with what would become the method that I continue to examine and develop even now, two presidencies later: The "guided seminar."

The Guided Seminar

I first learned about the guided seminar method from Dr. Lyndsay Agans, a professor in my master's program at the University of Denver. She assigned readings—so many readings!—each week, and we were placed in small groups to collaborate on those selections. The next class, we were asked to analyze the readings through thematic lenses—usually social, political, and economic. We would present for the benefit of our classmates, and then Dr. Agans would essentially cross-examine us. It felt authentic and accountable, and was perfect for me. I have always been an eager learner, and my favorite instructors have always been the ones who made me feel like I was in just a little over my head. Plus, I actually enjoy dialogue and discourse, which is a bonus for any prospective social studies teacher.

Eventually, my hunger for strong, contentious, honest, and dare-I-say "fun" discourse led to my colleague, Kevin Adams, and I founding the *Too Dope Teachers and a Mic* podcast in December 2016. We found that our most honest and motivating conversations happened not during staff meetings, but after. We both hungered for connection and conversation, and initially, our podcast was just us. Now, we can proudly say that we have hosted the likes of Dr. Gholdy Muhammad, rapper and filmmaker Boots Riley, and abolitionist pedagogue Dr. Bettina Love. The extent to which we have been blessed with community, discourse, and connection is profound and transformative. During our weekly Too Dope Teachers and a Mic podcast, we seek to "remix the conversation about race, power, and education," and our desire to learn and deepen our understanding of the world around us has only expanded.

But back to my classroom. An important step in its development was when I began to simply do share-outs. I would pose a thoughtful or thematic question as a "freestyle"—what basic folx call a "do-now"—and invite students to share.[7] The questions were argumentative and contentious by design, e.g., "Are people

---

[7] "Folx" is a word used to signal the inclusion of marginalized groups. For more, see *Merriam-Webster*, s.v. "folx," accessed March 15, 2022, https://bit.ly/3KG3lzq.

naturally good or evil?" "What does it mean to be free?" or "What is one thing you would change about the world?" Before long, these questions would constitute half the class period. Students were eager to share, and as I developed more equitable ways to promote sharing, students became even more engaged.

I next added an activity best represented by the work of mathematics trainer Annie Fetter, known as: "What do you notice? What do you wonder?" This method expanded the conversation, as well as the sources and texts we would use. "Notice-Wonder" was so engaging for students, that freestyle time (which was only supposed to occupy them for 10 percent of the class and allow me to take attendance) was taking up to 85 percent of class time. By the time we got to the planned activity, we had maybe ten minutes of the period left. I am certain that this created anxiety for the students, because I felt anxious. After even two days of this approach, we were precipitously behind, and my gradebook was a mess.

Finally, following an observation by an administrator, I was told "You ask really good questions!" They pointed to questions like "Tell me more about that," "How do you mean?" or "That's a really interesting point, so would you say…" The classroom dialogue was interesting and enjoyable. Relevant topics and connections were made, the discussion took different forms, and it always ended before students wanted it to.

Over the years, I have slowly committed to this as my only approach, or at least the one that defines what students experience in my classroom. Next, I will explain how my version of guided seminar could lead to classroom discussions that are impactful enough to perhaps have the possibility of transforming discourse in our society.

A Community of Thinkers

Most young people like to interact, discuss, debate, and become excitable. They want to feel something in their classes, and they want to feel that lessons and activities matter to teachers. While the system, with its focus on uniform measures, steers us toward a "teacher-proof" curriculum and instruction, students want something different. They want to be taught by a person who has passion for their subject, that is, a teacher who behaves as though the subject truly matters in real life. And sometimes just getting a little excitement in a classroom achieves this.

It is also of critical importance that teachers, especially social studies teachers, build relationships with their students. A teacher's views, personality, and approachability are constantly under scrutiny, particularly when it comes to history, government, injustices, etc. How is it possible to teach about democracy if our classrooms are undemocratic? How might we emphasize the "rule of law" while applying rules and consequences in an unjust or biased way? If we love what we do as social studies teachers, shouldn't we "practice what we preach"? And if we don't do so in the classroom, where else might students think the rules can be bent?

The Power of Questions

The key to successful classroom dialogue, especially around controversial topics, is to ask the right questions. This is, without a doubt, the most important skill I have developed as a teacher. Whether in a Socratic seminar or an expository writing prompt, you live or die by the questions you ask. The right questions can ignite energetic and engaged inquiry. The wrong questions, and even the right questions when poorly worded, can result in a soul-sucking "going-through-the-motions" conversation that keeps everyone feeling heavy and constantly checking the clock.

As earlier stated, I strive to create a space of healing and acceptance in my classroom. Students are encouraged to express themselves, and they are celebrated for taking risks. Sometimes that means voicing something in their hearts that may result in intense pushback and disagreement. The act of questioning helps me settle my heart rate so that I can engage with the class in an earnest and level-headed way. I do not get to decide what risks students take, and I also recognize that the absence of conflict does not equal harmony or trust.

I want to qualify the above with two statements. The first is that I try to ask questions of students before establishing my position. This is especially true if the person speaking has said something that is potentially inflammatory or triggering for me or the young people in my classroom.

My second qualification is that I also use this approach in most "real-life" situations, because I believe it is important to live our values and praxis, not just model them on the clock. So, if I find myself in a conversation with a family member, a guy at the bar, someone on the train or in a café, I bring the same approach. I want to understand their positions and motivations when speaking. I remind myself that no matter how shocking or incomprehensible their position is, it makes perfect sense to them. This position of theirs (which I may find derogatory, harmful, ignorant, or even hateful) is one at which they arrived through their lived experiences. So yes, even in the face of ignorance, I try to show empathy and respect. Note that I did not say kindness. But I do believe it is important that I support your humanity and respect that you are a real person with real-life experiences first and foremost.

Humanizing approaches to education have been researched and extensively published by scholars such as Dr. Maria del Carmen Salazar at the University of Denver. They have also been established through the foundational writings of Brazilian educator Paulo Freire. He described the practice of teaching as a "liberation" of consciousness, where the teacher serves not to insert or supplant consciousness into the minds of the students, but to activate their own consciousness.[8]

---

8 Denis Goulet, introduction to Paulo Freire, *Education for the Critical Consciousness* (New York: Continuum, 2007), vii-viii.

I would add from my own experiences that this framework assumes good-faith intellectual exploration, and it has been my experience that most young people, despite their parents or communities that influence them, do indeed seek authentic understanding. I have known my students to fall into conflict with other adults in their lives. This was not because I influenced them to believe a certain set of beliefs, but because I influenced them to believe themselves. Yet this approach of empathy has its limits, and the following anecdote outlines such a limitation.

The Hat

In the fall of 2021, when I was honored as the Colorado Teacher of the Year, I met with an individual from the Colorado Department of Education. We had arranged to meet to discuss one of my Teacher of the Year platform issues, which was to diversify the teacher development pipeline. (I have always approached my recognition as Colorado Teacher of the Year as a role in which I represent the 66,000 teachers in the state. I never let it become my own personal victory lap or ticker-tape parade.)

The state education professional and I decided to meet at a coffee shop near my school in central, downtown Denver. I love this neighborhood. There is a main drag that goes from Denver's industrial north side all the way to the southernmost suburbs, and one can see the entire city's identity along this route. Central Broadway has wealth, poverty, diversity, and small businesses. One need only walk a quarter mile to see social justice calls to protect Black lives, trans lives, immigrant lives, and others who find themselves at society's margins.

We had just sat down to talk when a man approached me in the coffee shop. He was middle-aged with long hair, a graying beard, wire-rimmed glasses, and—most notably—a red Make America Great Again (MAGA) hat. I inferred from his body language that he had left the house that day to stir things up. One does not simply don a MAGA hat and walk down Broadway with no expectation that they will gain attention.

I am similar. My own wardrobe invites conversation, and I have often invited my students and colleagues to "read me like a book." For example, on this particular day, I wore my "Abolitionist" T-shirt emblazoned with the following quote from Dr. Bettina Love's landmark book, *We Want to Do More than Just Survive*.[9]

Abolitionist Teaching
ab-o-li-tion-ist teach-ing
(Noun) The practice of working in solidarity with communities of color while drawing on the imagination, the creativity, the refusal, (re)membering, visionary thinking, healing, rebellious spirit, boldness, determination, and subversiveness of abolitionists to eradicate injustice in and outside of schools.

Mr. MAGA Hat approached me, and with no greeting or niceties, asked, "You know who the first abolitionists were, right?"

I've encountered this before as a popular talking point for some contemporary conservatives who wish to somehow paint themselves as more antiracist than perceived liberals. It's a game that I find boring, circular, and devoid of any historical context.

I responded, "Yup. Then what happened?"

He was puzzled. "When?"

I was direct and polite. "After."

I pointed out that as the Democratic Party became more racially progressive during the mid-20th century Civil Rights Movement, southern Democrats like Strom Thurmond, George Wallace, and other segregationists quit the party and became increasingly identified as or aligned with Republicans.

Mr. MAGA Hat's response to this sounded rehearsed, and his eyes never met mine as he spoke. I had read statements like the ones he was making in the vast apocalyptic wasteland that is the comments section of articles with a political focus. I tend to invite people to use their own words when discussing politics, not merely

9 Bettina L. Love, *We Want to Do More Than Survive Abolitionist Teaching and the Pursuit of Educational Freedom* (Boston: Beacon Press, 2019), 2.

parrot what others say. I realize this is common on all stations of the political spectrum, so I also try not to simply replicate what is said by people I find cool on social media. I wasn't sure what to make of him, but I knew that asking him my questions had brought my heart rate down and allowed me to keep some dignity during an inconvenient and frustrating moment.

To transition out of the exchange, I told him directly and politely, "Look, I would love to keep having this conversation, but I'm actually in a meeting. Have a great rest of your day!"

My guest from the Department of Education was aghast at the conversation, and had tears in her eyes. I apologized that she had to witness the interaction. "He probably didn't know," I joked, "that he was confronting the Colorado Teacher of the Year, who also happens to teach history." I shrugged, and the three of us went about our day.

So, here's the thing: Mr. MAGA Hat was an adult. I can push back against an adult by sharing facts, and I've been known to get into uncomfortable debates with people with whom my views did not align. But the classroom is an entirely different space for me. I am a teacher. I am responsible to my students for the course content, or the syllabus, and the curriculum. My students are not adults, and it is absolutely critical that they understand that history and politics are full of layers, complexity, and debate.

If a student raises their hand and asks: "Mr. Muñoz, did you know that Dr. King was a Republican?" I would answer quite differently than from the way I spoke to Mr. MAGA. In a situation with other adults, I am free to deploy my knowledge and understanding of history and politics, as I have experienced them. And while I can never be divorced from my lived experiences, with a young person, I can say: "I did know that! What do you all make of that fact?" I would then follow by walking students through the process of asking questions to deepen understanding.

The Necessity of Contentiousness

Even more important than the content of my class is the way that I approach the work, and how I encourage my students to approach it. In early 2021, I attended a keynote delivered by Dr. LaGarrett King, professor of education at the University of Missouri, where he also runs the Carter Center for Teaching African American History. A former educator who was on the traditional track to district-level leadership, Dr. King decided to focus on his training as a history teacher and deeply explore the ways in which history is taught in schools, particularly regarding Black history. He emphasized that engaging in Black historical consciousness is critical if we are to use history as the process of truth-telling and evidence gathering.

First, King argues that as we teach our political histories, we must acknowledge and name that "Black people were here before there was a United States, we have been here for the entire history of these United States, and we will be here after there is no longer a United States."[10] His humanizing pedagogy encourages us to consider the transcendent properties of history, especially as we share it, in all its complexity, with the next generations.

King's second point, which is profoundly meaningful to me, is that we must embrace the fact that history classes should be "contentious" in the recognition that every person who has lived is complex, contradictory, imperfect, and ultimately human. In this way, we reject the notion of topics that are off-putting or uncomfortable, regardless of contentious social and cultural dynamics around us.

For example, the Congo region was colonized by European powers, notably Belgium. But in modern times, the region was arguably recolonized by other Congolese people, like the military leader Mobutu Sese Seko (1965–1997). He proved to be a bad actor (to put it mildly), and amassed a fortune that, at the time of his death, dwarfed that of the Belgian King Leopold II. There is no

---

10 LaGarrett King, "Teaching Black History," (keynote address, Denver Public Schools meeting, Denver, CO, January 4, 2021).

"hot take" from this information, even if we agree that the bedrock of Africa's problems is still European exploitation. We must accept that the study of history, while rewarding and irreversible, will often leave us feeling unsatisfied and uncomfortable. It is from this discomfort that we can meaningfully examine multiple perspectives and work to shed light on agreed-on facts, and perhaps to arrive at larger truths.

As a teacher, I uncomfortably recall the ways in which I perpetuated harmful and even toxic approaches to history. In fairness to myself, I grew up longing for pleasant discourse and was never exposed to meaningful ways to address controversy or darkness in my history classroom. All I knew was my college experience taking ethnic studies courses, where I learned of historical traumas. That history of oppression put my own existence as a Brown boy into a larger context. So maybe the people in my community struggled not only because of their own choices, but also because of a social, political, and economic system that never gave us a chance? It was a system designed, at best, to maintain the status quo. At worst, the system seemed bound to eliminate us altogether.

As I mentioned earlier, in my first year teaching, I grew wary of situations that might put my job in jeopardy. But when I first entered teaching training, I was young and full of anger and disillusionment, determined to do what was never done for me. In my classroom, I would tell the truth, and give students the knowledge that was kept from them until now. But I quickly realized that the problem was much deeper than I expected.

A veteran teacher admonished me to avoid upsetting the students too much. She essentially told me that getting them angry and upset was dangerous, in the sense that they would not know what to do with their anger if I stoked it too much. Yet the students had become so alienated from the study of history that many of them "did not know what they did not know." For example, one day, I shared that the George Washington cherry tree story had never happened; it was a myth propagated to fuel the image of the so-called Founders as selfless visionaries who only wanted freedom for all Americans.

My students' response?

"What cherry tree?"

This unwelcome discovery shaped my classroom practice in probably the worst way possible. Instead of co-constructing historical knowledge with my students, I drew the conclusion that I needed to teach them "the basics," which I came to later realize was just code for the master narrative. I arrived at the conclusion that there was history they all needed to know before they would be able to learn their own histories.

I was 6 years into my career before I began to question my own practice. Who decided that this knowledge was worthy of preserving? What perspectives were not included, and therefore relegated to oblivion? (Answer: My own ancestors, among many others.) These nagging questions were cleverly hidden in the curriculum I taught, and the questions lingered even as I changed schools. I had only considered what the curriculum said my students needed to know. But now I was actively asking myself, "Why do the students need to know [this]?"

Of late, I have allowed myself to view the process of teaching, learning, and sharing history as a fluid and dynamic practice. This is a more radical deviation than I initially realized because decolonizing practices are disruptive to everything that is taught, learned, and assessed in traditional history classes.[11] As I embarked on this collision course with Western exceptionalism, my friend Diana, a brilliant history teacher in her own right, stated in a meeting that "history belongs to the people, not just in academia."

Those words are quotable and easily repeated. It's easy to imagine them emblazoned on T-shirts or contained in a worthy tweet. But that message is easier said than done. Teaching the spirit of history belonging to the people carries implications. An immediate one relates to textbooks. A classroom that democratizes the practice of history has little use for a single textbook. At their

---

11As defined by *Merriam-Webster*, decolonizing in this context means "to identify, challenge, and revise or replace assumptions, ideas, values, and practices that reflect a colonizer's dominating influence and especially a Eurocentric dominating influence."

most useful, textbooks are best deployed in the same way that a scholar deploys a dictionary, a thesaurus, or Google search. They list facts and brief summaries of events, but in most cases, do little to deepen, promote empathy or understanding, or position the lives of readers within a historical context. Some textbooks make this attempt, but it often falls flat for students as contrived and formulaic. Thus, the texts that are relevant are those which center the experiences of the students. This is to say nothing of the fact that students of color and from minoritized communities have been harmfully underrepresented and misrepresented in US textbooks.

So a declaration like "History belongs to the people" rings hollow if it is not accompanied by aligned praxis. In my teaching, I started to center stories rather than names, dates, and places. Additionally, I have invited students to act as producers of historical knowledge and insight, not just consumers of others' work. It means that we teachers are positioned to ensure that writing, reading, and speaking are authentic. It also means our students should be empowered to produce histories, rooted in their own experiences, families, and priorities.

I began to focus on the types of questions I asked in my classes. As noted, the questions we pose can either fuel or smother discourse, and they alter the whole energy of the learning space. For example, I was teaching a concurrent enrollment ethnic studies class in 2020. We had arrived at a discussion of Native American history and the present-day. Mind you, we were remote, and had just emerged from a quarantine. Students engaged differently than they did in person, or at least, mine engaged differently. But most of my students' cameras were still on, even if they pointed at the ceiling, and most students would unmute and share at times.

As an introduction to Native American history, I explained that my paternal grandmother was an Indigenous Person from the Mexican state of Oaxaca and that first language was likely not Spanish. I shared that though I do not consider myself an Indigenous Person, I am, like so many Latinx people, a descendant, in part, of the original people of the Americas.[12]

12 I learned via my younger sibling's "23 and Me" genetic testing results that we are roughly 40% Native American and only 10% Spanish/Iberian.

One of my students unmuted her microphone. "Mr. Muñoz," she said, "I think my grandma is Native American."

I replied, "I wouldn't be surprised; most of us Latinx people have some Indigenous background."

"Can I go ask her? She's in the next room."

"Of course!" I answered, excited about where this was going.

And then, we waited. The whole class was anxious to hear the results of their classmate's informal genealogical study.

After a couple of minutes, my student returned, breathless, holding a sticky note and her pencil. Reading from the yellow sticky note and pointing to the names with her pencil, she said, "Okay, so my grandma says …" Then my student read the names of three or four Indigenous groups, most of them from the American southwest and southwestern Mexico. Like my grandmother (and me), she had some Zapotec and Mixtec background.

And so we all bonded over space and distance.

The Tournament of Champions

Something similar happened during my AP World History class. For four years, I have had my students participate in what we called a Women in History Tournament of Champions, parallel to the NCAA's "March Madness" basketball tournament. It works this way: The students select a woman from history to research. She may be contemporary or from an era of the past. She may have relevance in any area of life, including, but not limited to, politics, literature, the arts, science, etc. The students research the life of the individual they selected, then they write a historically sound thesis statement, arguing their case to be named the winner of the title, "Champion among Champions." Once the students have completed their research, we create a giant bracket with 64 entries, each historical figure matched against another. The bracket is also made into an Excel document to be shared widely.

Finally, I make a Google Forms survey for participants to vote on each matchup. Since the bracket is randomly created, some matchups can be very exciting. One year, Rachel Carson, author of Silent Spring, a foundational text for the modern environmental movement, was matched against tennis legend Serena Williams. Williams got a lot of votes early, but soon voters were able to swing that matchup. In this way, the tournament is "played" along with the NCAA tournaments to capture some of the energy. One year, Olivia Meikle and Dr. Katie Nelson, co-hosts of the *What's Her Name* podcast, which tells stories of lesser-known women in history, joined us virtually to kick off the tournament with predictions, commentary, and analysis, and were easily more entertaining than analysts of most sports networks.

Again, I was forced by principle and my students to adjust my lesson as we went. First, I had to explain the fact that we were creating a literal tournament in which women would compete with each other. A few of my students and colleagues questioned this. Some pointed out that one mark of patriarchy is that women are forced to compete with each other, rather than stand in solidarity. My classroom community began by agreeing that all of the historical women we entered into the tournament were champions by virtue of making an impact on the lives around them. Though they lived in different places, different time periods, and came from different fields, we agreed that we would name our March Madness–style event the Tournament of Champions. This is similar to the FIFA World Cup Finals. The soccer spectacle that millions of us follow every four years is the culmination of a two-year playoff, and the 32 teams which play on the world's stage are already winners of their respective qualifying groups. We also agreed the real winners were the students and participants in our global vote, who would learn about the lives of at least 64 women from history. (I wonder how many adults are able to name 64 historical women?)

The next thing that was discussed was the term "March Madness." In our tournament's context, it almost seemed like a reference to when women's sanity had been questioned if they challenged convention, spoke up, or dared to be independent. So we removed any reference to it from our own tournament.

When I began this project in 2017, I generated a list of 70 historic women from antiquity to the 20th century. It included familiar names, such as Cleopatra, as well as lesser-known figures like Queen Teuta, the pirate-queen of Illyria. Some were European, like Joan of Arc, while others were Asian (Empress Dowager Cixi of the Qing dynasty), African (Nongqawuse of the Xhosa cattle-killing movement), and Latin American (Evita Perón of Argentina). I instructed the students to draw from my list and make their own entries, which they did with enthusiasm.

The winner of the inaugural Women in History Tournament of Champions was Harriet Tubman. This came after a two-week process which began in my classroom, expanded to the entire school, and later, an untold number of social media accounts. The students began to grasp the excitement of the tournament gradually. First, the only votes came from the classes I was teaching. Shortly after, other students in the school made their way to my classroom during office hours, lunch, and before and after school, asking if they could vote.

When my students learned that students and teachers outside of our class were voting, they became more excited and committed to the tournament. One student, I am told, leveraged every social media platform on which she was active to get votes. Another openly campaigned at lunch and in homeroom. I felt some anxiety reading off the votes every couple of days, because it was all the students wanted to know. I was particularly pleased that all four quarter-finalists—Rosa Parks, Katherine Johnson, Frida Kahlo, and Tubman—were women of color. This was very much a reflection of student discussions that happened in our AP World History class around representation of people of color.

As the tournament went on, the students found that they needed to research each person to make a determination, especially by the semifinals, when a hairsbreadth of distinction separated the exceptional individuals listed above. In addition, the students were asked to take potentially contentious positions as a part of this project. If even in their own minds, they had to make a decision between four incredible women, they had to do some hard thinking, requiring rigorous thought and analysis. I also took care to make the prize something fun. The student winner of the tournament received a poorly-photoshopped picture of himself with Tubman.

COVID-19 hit us like a freight train as we prepared for the 2020 tournament, but even in our initial planning stages, disruptive questions emerged. Right before the shutdowns and quarantines, one student asked if they could enter Marsha P. Johnson, a transgendered activist who played a prominent role in the Stonewall Uprising of 1969. I approved. My goal was not to prepare my students for a question on Johnson on the AP World History exam—although I imagine Johnson could be referenced in an essay. I wanted to show my students how young people can actively participate in the production and peer-review of historical scholarship and narrative. If what they discover and share is not in the curriculum, well, then perhaps the curriculum should change. After all, the word curriculum comes from the Latin for "action of running, course of action."[13] It suggests dynamism and fluidity. In a very real way, I had arrived at a moment where the "curriculum" was emerging and moving, representing our moment and those past concurrently.

This became a significant shift. Contentious and controversial topics emerged more organically. As students selected women to highlight, research, and promote in the tournament, questions emerged and debates ensued. There was a question whether a transgendered individual should be a part of the tournament. There was a question whether Meghan Markle should really be considered as a champion of history. "Does my entry need to be famous?" "Can she still be alive?" "What if she was famous for something bad?" All of these questions disrupted my own notions of "proper historical study" and I am grateful that they did.

As the Women in History Tournament of Champions evolved, I decided to let the students choose their own women, and my class was fired up at the prospect. They entered women from Hypatia, the 4th-century Greek philosopher and mathematician, to Ellen DeGeneres. We all learned so much more about the history of women throughout the world. Before this particular year, I had never even heard of revolutionary socialist Rosa Luxembourg, Gladys Bentley of the Harlem Renaissance, Princess

---

13*Merriam-Webster*, s.v. "curriculum," accessed April 11, 2022, https://bit.ly/3vca3H0.

Zhao of Pingyang, or numerous other fascinating figures. Both my knowledge and theirs was deepened, and the list of women we created became more representative of my classroom communities and the historical moments we were navigating.

The tournament did not happen in 2020, as it was derailed by COVID-19. But the following year, still quarantined most of the year, we tried again. This time, a different student asked me an unexpected question in class: "Can I enter my grandma?" This was new, and I hesitated. I was thinking, Here, I gave you all kinds of choices, but now you want to go even more outside the boundaries?

"Tell me about your grandma," I asked the student.

"Well, I don't know, she went through a lot, and I think she accomplished a lot even though she wasn't well-known. She just inspires me."

"How much do you know about her?"

"I know where she lived and my mom and some family members have some crazy stories about her."

"Do you think you could also try to connect her life to that time in history? Like did global events impact her life?"

"I don't know. I can try?"

Working together in a challenging journey, we discovered that the student's grandmother, Julia, who was about the same age as my own mother, left home at the age of 15. From a rural community in Kansas, Julia wanted to escape the provincialism and tension of her small and very religious community. She encountered violence, homelessness, hunger, and abuse. But she persevered and became the wise matriarch of the family, and vowed that nothing like this would ever happen to her descendants.

The story is inspiring, but one may rightly ask, "So how did this become a historical research project?"

The answer is through the formation of research questions. We looked into religious movements of the 1960s and 1970s, and found that there were at least three religious movements, studied by Amy Hart, that unsettled traditional religious communities, particularly after World War II. I helped my student write questions to ask her grandmother that would ascertain whether there was a connection between Julia's flight and these movements. The student came back to me with responses, and as may be expected, Julia didn't remember much, saying that she didn't know why the church was suddenly intolerant and strict, just that it was and that she had to get out of there. Through the process, my student learned that history is often unresolved. We were not able, in the brief time she had to research, to definitively determine how Julia's running away fit into the bigger picture of doctrinal tension in Midwestern Christianity during the 1960s and 1970s, but we could make some educated guesses based on the historical context.

We also learned to treat historical subjects with sensitivity and empathy. At one point, Julia reflectively asked her granddaughter, "I just don't know why anyone would want to read about my life," further emphasizing that every living person is a history unto themselves, and that the notion that there are unimportant people in history robs us of its humanity. And yet this is what the traditional methods of history (with its names, dates, places, events, and rote memorization) does.

Through this question-and-answer process, I pushed my student to think and consider not whether she was allowed to interpret history in this manner but how she would do it. This was an epiphany for me. History belongs to the people. It's just about cultivating a willingness among young people to assert their place in it. Not everyone is able to complete a complex genealogy, but most students can gather stories of family members, grandparents, and even great-grandparents who also have stories.

Here's a contentious question for social studies teachers: Does it truly matter whether students know the taxation issues raised at the Second Continental Congress? Or, at the very least, does it matter as much as what their grandmothers survived? My grandmother ran off to Los Angeles during the Great Depression and had what I've been told was the best time ever. Her independent actions at the age of 17 were such an anomaly, given the time. And her life, which confronted the world that had been constructed around her in unapologetic ways, provides me with more insight into what it meant to be a person in the world at that time than any textbook.

What if we had an entire class dedicated to "The History of Our Grandmothers"? Or "A History of the House We Grew Up In," or even "The History of the Records and Eight-Tracks in My Dad's Stereo When I Was a Kid"? No matter the topic, it can be unlocked with good questions, and the right questions will reveal whole worlds to us. Good research should leave us with more questions than answers.

Signal Fires

In this time of uncertainty, frustration, fear, suspicion, and global trauma, healing requires a return to self. Rather than try to agree on a single version of history that excludes some and excuses others, we must claim our own stories and those of our ancestors. This calls for a shift in instruction, and the shift that I propose is one that centers the principles of autonomy, storytelling, and self-determination. This shift helps our students become the historians and storytellers of their communities. The students have lived through a profound historical trauma, and this experience has left them feeling isolated, unseen, and anonymous. But storytelling and research can give them a sense of self-determination that might not exist in the traditional classroom, which places them at an arms' length from what makes history great: the feeling of connection to the past.

The specifics of this project may include some existing practices, including local history, oral history, popular history, or something new that still has not revealed itself. The difference is that these innovative practices have always lived on the periphery, projects we could do if "we get through" the content. I propose that what was marginalized become front-and center, and the result would be an approach that will manifest differently in every learning space.

By the end of the fateful 2019–2020 school year, the AP World History curriculum was cleaved by more than 100 years. Due to the barriers erected by the pandemic, the College Board made the decision to remove all content post-1900 from the exam. Students would only complete one essay on an event that occurred before the dawn of the 20th century. That's before any world war, before the Cold War, before decolonization or civil rights, before globalization. My students, who had been excited to connect past to present, were left with a sudden, abrupt, and insensitive end to the course. So much for the sanctity of the timeline.

So for our class's AP final project, I instructed students to identify a topic, development, or story of their choice from history. It could be an event or person that they looked forward to learning about, or it could be a topic that was not covered in class but that they believed should have been. The students completed interesting, sound research projects on LGBTQIA+ history, K-Pop, military technology, espionage, soccer, and many more subjects that I could never have formulated on my own. The work was far from perfect, but we all learned to engage the historical process that is authentic, heartfelt, and relevant, and I emerged with new insights on how to re-imagine history instruction in secondary schools. For while these specific strategies and practices have existed in isolated and additive ways for years, they have never formed the center of history education.

The students asked to compile their stories, and so we did. We decided to title it *Roads Untraveled*. The title encapsulates the past, present, and future that we experienced all at once in the spring of 2020. The journey to find their own voice and likeness in history was new. Attempting to learn world history during a catastrophic pandemic is a road untraveled. The opportunities to learn deeply and in community in person was a road they never got to travel with me. And what lies ahead is a road untraveled.

But what ties this labyrinthine set of stories together, from the historic Obama inauguration to the COVID-19 pandemic, is that concept of roads untraveled. Since I started teaching in 1999, I have seen that students have wanted autonomy, and that traditional approaches to teaching history prevented their autonomy. They instead have been forced to endure antiquated practices that ignore their perspectives and places in history and community.

My journey along this road started with a singular light, which was the voices of my students: the hunger they had to be heard, seen, respected, and remembered. That light has guided me along a sometimes dark and lonely road, with occasional signal fires along the way. But more than two decades later, the untraveled road is the only one I know.

Gerardo A. Munoz is a writer, poet, and doctoral student who was Colorado's 2021 Teacher of the Year. Over his 22-year career, Gerardo has worked to engage student voices and promote colleague solidarity. He cohosts the podcast Too Dope Teachers and a Mic with Kevin Adams and hosts the podcast Habitually Disruptive. He is a seven-time Distinguished Teacher, National History Teacher of the Year nominee, winner of the Colorado Education Association's 2021 Golden Apple Award, and winner of the Take's 2021 Black History Malcolm X Award. Muñoz is currently at work on his first book.

CHAPTER 4

Primary Considerations: Navigating Sensitive History with Younger Students

Kelly Reichardt
Howard County Public School System, Maryland

In the courtroom of human events, primary sources act as evidence and expert witnesses, providing intimate glimpses into the past for all students. However, primary sources can sometimes be false, forged, mistranslated, misappropriated, or simply lost to history. As such, social studies students and their teachers must know how to properly identify, appraise, and handle these sources with the same care as a curator.

In this chapter, Kelly Reichardt explains how teachers can go about using primary sources with some of the best resources available—including some of her own design.

A shouting match in a school's drop-off line. The heckling of public officials at a school board meeting. Threats directed at teachers and administrators. Sadly, there has been an increase in stories similar to these in recent years. According to a 2019 Pew Research survey, 85 percent of Americans feel the tone and nature of political debate has become more negative in the United States over the past several years.[1] A subsequent study found that people in the United States are far more divided than those in 17 other nations with similar economies. About 90 percent of US adults saw significant conflicts between people of different political parties, nearly twice that of the overall countries' median score. And roughly seven in 10 Americans reported more conflict between people of varying racial or ethnic backgrounds, more than any other nation surveyed.[2]

In consequence, "civil discourse"—defined as an exchange to enhance understanding while fostering positive interactions—has become increasingly harder to attain. Having a civil discourse does not mean all parties reach an agreement. Rather, civil conversations are based on honesty, empathy, and require participants to be open to a constructive exchange of ideas. Without these common courtesies, agreeing to disagree is just impossible.

How do we break our cycles of discordant and dysfunctional communication? How can we learn to approach controversial topics that foster a healthy and respectful exchange of ideas? Most importantly, how do we ensure our children are able to apply critical thinking strategies when approaching potentially contentious and argumentative topics, both in and out of the classroom?

According to Dr. Diana Hess, dean of University of Wisconsin at Madison's School of Education, "when schools fail to teach students how to engage with controversial political and constitutional issues—or worse, suppress, ignore, or exclude such

1 "Public Highly Critical of State of Political Discourse in the U.S.," Pew Research Center, April 12, 2021, https://pewrsr.ch/3O8d6IX.

2 "Americans See Stronger Societal Conflicts Than People in Other Advanced Economies," Pew Research Center, October 13, 2021, https://pewrsr.ch/3nvjzCn.

issues from the curriculum—they send a host of destructive and misguided messages."[3]

By avoiding highly charged issues, educators send a message that these topics are not important to their students—or that their students are not capable of thinking critically about them. We need to teach our students how to have civil conversations at a young age, and elementary school is an ideal time to grow empathy, civility, and higher-order thinking skills.

Incorporating the use of primary and secondary sources into daily classroom lessons is an excellent way to approach hot button topics. The opportunity to investigate and examine sources can maximize student agency, pique curiosity, and encourage student-initiated exploration. Photographs, political cartoons, children's trade books, maps, and ephemera are all excellent resources to encourage discussion, foster critical analysis skills, and allow students to draw their own conclusions about historical events.

Using Photographs

A picture is a powerful way for students to enhance their observational and interpretive skills. Not only can they spur discussion and engage student agency, but pictures are also primary sources. They are records. They are incriminating. They are ways the past can instantly communicate pain and injustices across the centuries.

Civil Rights Movement

The modern US Civil Rights Movement began in the 1950s and continues to the present day. For teachers covering objectives and standards dealing with civic participation and democratic freedoms, the Civil Rights Movement has a plethora of visually dramatic moments for students to explore. From the 1960 Greensboro, North Carolina, sit-ins to today's Black Lives Matter protests, photos and videos can bring this movement to life.

---

3 Diana E. Hess, "Teaching Controversial Issues: An Introduction," *Social Education* 82, no. 6 (2018): 306.

When staging a photo analysis activity on the Civil Rights Movement, it is important for students to have a contextual understanding of the photo. The intent of this article is not to review civil rights history, but as context, abolitionists and free and enslaved African Americans had called for equality and civil rights long before the Civil War. Although the 13th, 14th, and 15th Amendments abolished slavery and promised citizenship and voting rights, Black Americans continued to be denied civil rights due to Jim Crow laws, which dominated governments in the southeastern United States from 1865 to 1965. Black individuals were disenfranchised and subjected to discrimination, racism, violence, and even murder by white supremacists acting with impunity for decades—and students need to see evidence of this in some form to make it relevant and understand its gravity.

Many photographs and videos from civil rights events are available online at the Library of Congress and the National Archives Records Administration. For example, the "First March From Selma" digital collection from the Library of Congress contains a particularly powerful image of Alabama state troopers attacking the marchers during the event, which became known as Bloody Sunday.[4] One helpful way to introduce students to investigating these images is by utilizing the Primary Source Analysis Tool from the Library of Congress.[5] The first time this is shared with the class, teachers should model the observe, reflect, and question format recommended by the Library of Congress.

Teachers can ask questions—such as those noted here—to guide student observations of photo details, per the Library of Congress guide.[6]

- Where does your eye go first?
- What do you see that you didn't expect?
- What powerful words and ideas are expressed?

4 "Today in History - March 7," Library of Congress, https://bit.ly/3rmXPKl.

5 "Getting Started with Primary Sources," Library of Congress, https://bit.ly/3JDQKvc.

6 Ibid.

Other questions can guide student reflections and personal responses, including:

- What feelings and thoughts does the primary source trigger in you?
- What questions does it raise?

More open-ended inquiries can serve as a closing activity, such as:

- What was happening during this time period?
- What was the creator's purpose in making this primary source?
- What does the creator do to get his or her point across?
- What was this primary source's audience?
- What biases or stereotypes do you see?

Gilded Age Tenements

When teaching classes on sensitive subjects, such as economic inequality and classism, a teacher might choose to highlight the treatment of the poor during the Gilded Age (1870–1900). Photography played a pivotal role in exposing unsanitary and dangerous urban housing arrangements that are shocking by modern standards.

After the Civil War, it is estimated that 24 million people moved to American cities.[7] Jacob Riis, a Danish immigrant, became a crime reporter for the *New York Tribune* in 1873. He was assigned to New York's Lower East Side, a neighborhood riddled with crime, disease, and poverty. It was considered one of the most densely populated places on earth.

Riis believed that if he could expose the nation to the squalid conditions and high crime rates in the Lower East Side's tenements, change would happen and support would come. He wanted to run images with his writing, which led him to explore the new technology of flash photography. With these photos, Riis was able to show the unsafe, unsanitary conditions experienced by children living in tenements. His writings and photographs reveal the lack of windows, ventilation, and green-space in these dwellings.

7 Philip Martin, "Trends In Migration To The U.S.," May 19, 2014, *PRB*, https://bit. ly/37DH0E2.

As Riis's news articles, drawings, and photographs appeared in New York City newspapers, he also conducted a series of public presentations where he shed light on the horrors faced by those living in tenement housing. These lectures included a lantern slideshow, where he used early technology to project his photos on a screen or wall. He turned those lecture notes into a book titled *How the Other Half Lives*, which included his observations, interviews, drawings, and statistics he compiled in collaboration with the New York City Health Department. The popular book also featured unsettling descriptions that opened the public's eyes to the harsh realities of the city slums.

A digital collection of Riis's work can be found at the Library of Congress and the Museum of the City of New York.[8] One way to introduce students to investigating photographic images is by utilizing a Preview & Post activity. This allows students time to observe an individual image in the preview stage and then note questions they have about the image in the post stage. "Preview & Post" is my version of the "Sticky Note Solution" found in the Teaching with the Library of Congress collection.[9]

Teachers should display the selected Riis images in class as digital displays or printed hard copies. Then they divide the class into groups, provide them with sticky notes, and instruct the class to observe the image independently; consider allowing four to five minutes per image.

Next, students should leave a sticky note with a question they have about each corresponding image. Remind students that when observing these photographs, they should also spend time thinking about what actions are taking place, what text appears, and if there are any clues about the time or place of the photo.

Repeat the Preview & Post procedures, allowing time for students to visit each image and post their questions. Teachers can facilitate a class discussion based on the questions that were posted, allowing other students to provide possible answers.

8 "Jacob A. Riis," Museum of the City Of New York, https://bit.ly/3Jzs2MK; "Jacob A. Riis," Museum of the City Of New York, https://bit.ly/3Jzs2MK.

9 Cheryl Lederle, "Observation in Primary Source Analysis: The Sticky Notes Solution," Library of Congress, August 21, 2012, https://bit.ly/3uzatlf.

Employing a Preview & Post strategy gives students the chance to take ownership of their learning because they are able to create the questions that will drive the class discussion. Additionally, this strategy provides an opportunity for increased student agency by ensuring their voice is heard.

The activity leans on student-directed learning with the teacher in the facilitator, not lecturer, role. Preview & Post could be used in a variety of stages during the lesson. For example, when introducing a new topic, this strategy could be an effective motivation tool. Alternatively, Preview & Post could also serve as a formative assessment to gather a pulse on students' understanding.

Peaceful Protest by Athletes

The First Amendment guarantees the right of every citizen to exercise their freedom of speech. From *Tinker v. Des Moines Independent Community School District* (1969) to *Mahanoy Area School District v. B.L.* (2021), free speech has been a contested issue for adults and students alike. Yet when athletes take a political or social stance, it has led to heated debates over when it is appropriate for notable private citizens to speak out, protest, or participate in acts of civil disobedience. Teachers might use their students' familiarity with sports to make politically and emotionally charged subjects (such as debates over free speech) more accessible and familiar.

Teachers can trace athlete's peaceful protests to illustrate civic participation and historical causation standards. Begin this activity by providing students with case studies on a few examples of athlete-led protests. Consider putting together a collection of images and background for each case study; suggested case studies include the 1968 Olympics, #takeaknee, and the Women's National Basketball Association (WNBA) and 2020 Olympic protests.

Perhaps the most prominent athletic protest seen in the 20th century occurred at the 1968 Olympic games. As the US anthem played at the medal presentation, sprinters Tommie Smith and John Carlos raised a closed fist Black Power salute. This protest was meant to draw attention to human rights, and was also a call for more coaching positions for Black Americans. As a result, Smith and Carlos received jeers and even death threats.

Now fast-forward to 2016, when Colin Kaepernick, quarterback for the San Francisco 49ers, sat during the national anthem to protest police brutality and racial injustice against people of color. The #takeaknee movement began when Kaepernick and like-minded players protested by kneeling during the national anthem during the 2016–2017 National Football League (NFL) season. The gesture received mixed reactions from players and the public, particularly after then President Trump expressed anger over it. Television networks cut away from the protests during their live broadcasts. The NFL owners ruled that players could no longer kneel during the anthem without consequences.

It was not until after the 2020 murder of George Floyd and an explosive summer of national unrest that the NFL issued a statement that they were wrong to oppose their players' peaceful protest.

No professional US sports league has been more active and organized than the members of the WNBA in their social protests. Additionally, Olympic athletes protested at the 2020 Olympic Games (which took place in 2021 due to the COVID-19 pandemic), calling attention to issues including Black Lives Matter, the unequal treatment of the LGBTQIA+ community, and the need to increase awareness of mental health issues. Athletes are public figures with a vast audience of fans and social media followers. Their political protests draw ire from some while others defend this First Amendment right.

For an activity on athletes and the First Amendment, students can select an athlete or group of athletes involved in a protest. Teachers may provide background on the protest or allow students time to research this themselves. Students will then complete a Sensory Figure activity by taking on the perspective of the athlete and guiding others through their subject's personality and passion.

There are many Sensory Figures templates that can be found online; many versions have the students focus on what the individual would wear or look like. I created the Sensory Figure graphic organizer that appears in this book—with graphic support from my son—to draw out more emotional connections such as thoughts, feelings, fear, and pride.

This activity can provide students with an opportunity to critique arguments as well as build empathy. Students will answer questions about what the athlete felt, feared, accomplished, and who their protest might have inspired.

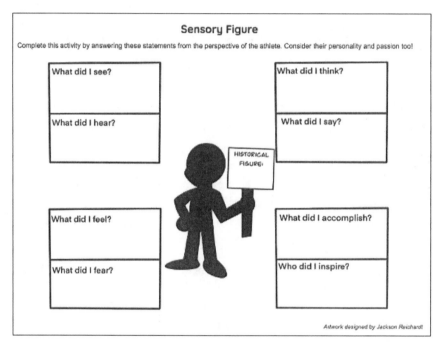

Graphic by Kelly Reichardt and Jackson Reichardt. Full-page version in Appendix II.

Using Political Cartoons

Political cartoons offer unique ways to easily capture students' attention because they typically offer amusing or critical critiques of their time period. Their subjects may include political opinions, widespread public criticisms, or the missteps by individuals in the public spotlight.

These cartoons usually incorporate symbolism and exaggeration to capture one's attention and convey their messages, which is evident in the famous Benjamin Franklin political cartoon, Join or Die.

The first American political cartoon appeared in Franklin's newspaper, *The Pennsylvania Gazette*, on May 9, 1754.[10]

It was a call to unite the colonies during the French and Indian War. The political cartoons that followed offer us a window into public sentiment in the past, allowing students to make their own interpretations and draw conclusions after analyzing the cartoon and its historical context.

10 Benjamin Franklin, "Join or Die," cartoon, *The Pennsylvania Gazette*, May 9, 1754, from Library of Congress Prints and Photographs Division, https://www.loc.gov/item/2002695523/.

Standing Rock Sioux

Consider using political cartoons to cover the Dakota Access Pipeline protests of 2016–2017 as a way to address democratic principles, rules and laws, economic decision-making, and human-environmental interactions. *Indian Country Today*, an Indigenous digital news outlet, provides a timeline of events that occurred with regard to the pipeline.[11] For a balanced investigation, teachers may also share background information provided by the pipeline owner, Energy Transfer Partners, from their official website.[12] This topic may resonate with youth because middle school students who are members of the Standing Rock Sioux Tribe and the Cheyenne River Sioux Tribe started the Sacred Stone Camp.[13] Teachers could present this fact as an example of students taking action and participating in our democracy by exercising their First Amendment rights.

Media outlets, such as the *Star Tribune* or *Arizona Republic*, and political cartoon websites provide a number of resources to review with a class.[14] Consider conducting a web search for "Standing Rock Sioux political cartoon."

After locating an appropriate image, guide students through the process of analyzing a political cartoon using TACOS (Time, Action, Captions, Objects, and Symbols). This activity has been used by social studies educators for many years.[15] The TACOS activity helps students investigate cartoons by unpacking their elements. Students may need guidance in identifying what objects may symbolize.

11 Kolby KickingWoman, "Dakota Access Pipeline Timeline," *Indian Country Today*, last modified July 9, 2020, https://bit.ly/37JAGuz.

12 "Dakota Access Pipeline Facts," Energy Transfer LP, https://daplpipelinefacts.com.

13 Saul Elbein, "The Youth Group That Launched a Movement at Standing Rock," *New York Times*, January 31, 2017, https://nyti.ms/3rhiiAg.

14 Steve Sack, "Sack Cartoon: Dakota Access Pipeline and Standing Rock," cartoon, *Star Tribune*, November 2, 2016, http://strib.mn/3796FES; Steve Benson, "Benson: Standing Rock Isn't over Yet," cartoon, *Arizona Republic*, December 5, 2016, https://bit.ly/3LYsSUF.

15 Megan Nieman, "Tacos Anyone?," *Doing Social Studies* (blog), May 24, 2013, https://bit.ly/3E8hzqn.

I created the TACOS: Analyzing a Political Cartoon graphic organizer to help students record their observations.[16] This activity would benefit from a collaborative learning arrangement, such as Think-Pair-Share. Teachers can guide student analysis by asking the following guiding questions:

> **Time:** When was the cartoon created? What is the setting?
>
> **Action:** Describe what you see happening.
>
> **Caption:** What is the text or dialogue within the cartoon? Is there a title of the cartoon?
>
> **Objects:** List everything you see. Characters, items, scenery, etc.
>
> **Symbols:** Do you see any images that are symbols?

Environmental Movements: Then and Now

Our actions on addressing or ignoring environmental issues have been a contested issue for elected officials and private citizens alike. In order to trace our changing views, teachers may consider showcasing environmental political cartoons over the course of several decades. Early national conservation efforts can be traced to President Theodore Roosevelt (1901–1909) and John Muir, who is often called America's first environmentalist. Muir co-founded the Sierra Club to ensure protection of America's natural resources and parks. While Muir is credited with the campaign of preserving America's natural spaces for future generations, his legacy is now being reexamined for his harmful stereotypes and racist views; this provides another outlet to discuss a hot button issue with students.

Provide students with background information on the modern conservation movement that began in 1962 when US marine biologist Rachel Carson published Silent Spring. Trace the series of environmental disasters that occurred in the 1960s and the grassroots conservation organizations that sprouted all over the country as a result.

---

16 Kelly Reichardt, TACOS: Analyzing a Political Cartoon, August 12, 2019, Baltimore, MD.

Another way to introduce students to investigating political cartoons is by guiding them in contextualizing the image.[17] This is the act of placing events in a proper context, thus allowing students to identify patterns and themes in a particular historical time period.

After you provide hard copies of cartoons at stations or via a shared drive, students should be asked to locate the image in time and place, and challenged to determine its antecedents, intended audience, and overall message. Teachers should guide this illustrative contextualization lesson by asking:

- When was the political cartoon created?
- Who was the intended audience?
- Where was the political cartoon published?
- What was happening at the time of the publishing?
- How was the United States and the world different then?
- How was the United States and the world the same?
- What is the cartoon's message?
- How might the circumstances in which the political cartoon was created affect its content?

By selecting political cartoons that span a number of years, students should be encouraged to identify patterns of how opinions on a host of subjects may or may not have changed over time. Additionally, students may be moved to higher-order thinking skills by making predictions about which historical events might have contributed to the cartoon's creation and how this may have impacted the artist's mindset. Encourage students to question each other's interpretations of the political cartoons.

---

17 Cartoons are available online at the Library of Congress and the National Archives Records Administration. One possible example to share with students is an online exhibit at the Library of Congress titled "Down to Earth," which is dedicated to the work of US political cartoonist Herbert Block; "Down to Earth: Herblock and Photographers Observe the Environment Exhibition Home," Library of Congress, September 22, 2012, https://bit. ly/3E6Vete.

Global Warming vs. Climate Change

Let's unpack what climate change and global warming are. The National Aeronautics and Space Administration's Jet Propulsion Laboratory provides excellent descriptions of both in an online FAQ which defines global warming as the "well-documented" and "long-term warming of the planet … since the early 20th century and most notably since the late 1970s."[18] It then specifies that climate change:

> … encompasses global warming, but refers to the broader range of changes that are happening to our planet. These include rising sea levels; shrinking mountain glaciers; accelerating ice melt in Greenland, Antarctica and the Arctic; and shifts in flower/plant blooming times. These are all consequences of warming, which is caused mainly by people burning fossil fuels and putting out heat-trapping gasses into the air.[19]

Definitions of these two topics varies, which can lead to confusion about and controversy over its effects; deliberate misinformation from the oil industry and some political leaders only further muddies the water. As a result, educators should note the differences between global warming and climate change, and present them with the highest confidence and authority. In short, when examining global warming, focus on the Earth's rise in temperature over time. But when discussing climate change, emphasize the rise in temperature alongside the myriad physical changes to the planet, such as melting polar ice caps and eroding coastlines.

There are many climate change connections to social studies. Students could examine the impact of climate change and the increase of severe weather events on geography and economics. Allow space for discussions on how drought affects crops, food prices, and the availability of fresh drinking water; how rising sea levels impact

18 "What's the Difference Between Climate Change and Global Warming?," NASA, October 9, 2014, https://go.nasa.gov/3O4NiNM.

19 Ibid.

housing around the world; or how wildfires threaten endangered species' habitats, air quality, and human life. Topics such as reliance on fossil fuels, pollution in developing and developed countries, and the diplomacy required for solutions such as the Paris Agreement are all ripe for class discussions and have a direct connection to social studies curriculum.

Students could also identify human actions that have environmental consequences to cover human-environmental interaction standards. The American Museum of Natural History in New York has an excellent online climate change resource for teachers and students.[20] Additionally, *National Geographic* offers a plethora of background information to support student investigation, such as videos, maps and graphics, interactive quizzes, and even an interview with Leonardo DiCaprio on a documentary he produced on global warming, *Before the Flood* (2016).[21]

Political cartoons are a terrific tool for introducing global warming to students. In addition to the Library of Congress's digital "Down to Earth" exhibit, a web search will yield environmental-themed cartoons from mainstream media outlets. Teachers can sharpen online searches by employing a variety of search operator tools. For example, using quotation marks around a word or phrase will show results of the exact word or phrase within the quotations. Using a "+" sign states that results must include the word preceded by the plus sign. Using "filetype:jpg" will find results of only .jpgs.

After locating an appropriate image, guide students through the process of examining a political cartoon by using the Political Cartoon Analysis worksheet from the National Archives and Records Administration.[22] *US News & World Report* has a great collection of digital climate change political cartoons as well.[23]

20 "Climate Change Resources," American Museum Of Natural History, March 25, 2015, https://bit.ly/365lRCb.

21 "Global Warming - National Geographic Search," *National Geographic*, https://on.natgeo.com/3LVIqZm.

22 "Analyze a Cartoon," National Archives and Records Administration, December 4, 2019, https://bit.ly/3rjzFQQ.

23 "Cartoons on Climate Change and Global Warming," *US News & World Report*, December 10, 2021, https://bit.ly/3M0B5b6.

As before, teachers can ask questions to guide student observations on the cartoons, such as:

- What do you notice first?
- What words are visible (title, caption, text)?
- What people or places do you see?
- What activities are taking place?
- What emotions are portrayed?
- What symbols do you see, and what do they mean?
- What is the message?

According to the Iris Center at Vanderbilt University, the suggested wait time after each question is three to five seconds.[24] Increased wait time will allow for more students to formulate an answer and gather confidence to share.

With the Political Cartoon Analysis worksheet or any other strategy, an excellent informal wrap-up might be asking students where they can learn more about the events portrayed in this image. In this way, students are taking control of extending their own learning. Teachers might prompt students by asking the following questions:

- Where can you find this image?
- What words should I enter into a search engine?
- Which websites should I visit?
- Where can I find similar illustrations or other illustrations from the same cartoonist?
- How can I determine the date it was printed?

---

24 The IRIS Center, Fundamental Skill Sheet: Wait Time (Nashville, TN: Vanderbilt University, 2018), https://bit.ly/3JwxmAh.

Maps and Ephemera

While maps appear in almost any social studies textbook, technology now offers students the opportunity to investigate both static and animated maps from varying time periods, competing cartographers, and with seemingly endless filter options. These visuals can complement geography standards and be used to trace human population patterns, the global economy, and human-environment interactions objectives.

Spatial reasoning and visual learning are additional benefits when incorporating maps, making them handy accessories to any social studies classroom—especially since students might already be familiar with maps from pirate movies, board games, video games, and high fantasy entertainment. Be mindful of age appropriate choices particularly for movies and video games. Teachers should utilize these whenever possible to make map-based lessons more accessible and engaging. (It's not every day that a student might use their knowledge of *Pirates of the Caribbean* or *Legend of Zelda: Breath of the Wild* to help their fellow classmates learn how to read a map!) Teachers may take this further with problem solving activities or tantalizing tidbits to pique their students' curiosity, such as by showcasing the unexplored regions of older maps, rapidly changing animated wartime maps, or even *hic sunt dracones* ("Here be dragons").

Maps also impact the way we view our place in the world, so great care should be taken to avoid perpetuating past misconceptions. The Mercator map, for example, is one of the most egregious examples of "map bias" in recent history due to how it distorts certain land masses. Students should be allowed to explore different types of maps to make comparisons and chip away at map bias.[25]

---

25 Betsy Mason, "Why Your Mental Map Of The World Is Wrong," *National Geographic*, November 16, 2018, https://on.natgeo.com/3uAhPv4.

Native Lands Map

As the United States wrestles with racial injustice, many states have passed legislation to require Indigenous history and culture in social studies curricula. Other states, such as South Dakota and Texas, are being criticized for "white-washing" their curricula to seemingly erase mention of Native Americans.[26] This despite the fact that the United States Department of the Interior released a 2022 report revealing that tens of thousands of Indigenous children died in the custody of federal Indian boarding schools. These children had been forced to the schools as part of an official US assimilation policy stripped Native American children of their languages and cultures.

Grappling with these tragic examples of racial injustice can be difficult and painful for any educator, but examining the past and boldly addressing past atrocities is necessary for our students to build a better future, correct past and present misconceptions, disprove stereotypes, and expose injustices.

A useful tool recommended for any educator covering this subject is Native Land Digital, an online resource offered by an Indigenous-led Canadian nonprofit. Their interactive map helps students recognize the ancestral lands of Indigenous Peoples. Students can explore Indigenous territories, languages, and treaties for locations around the world.[27]

Native Land Digital also provides a useful "Teacher's Guide" to support the incorporation of their resources in lessons.[28] Teachers can allow time for students to simply explore this map as a motivational activity, perhaps by entering their school's address for a brief lesson on local Indigenous history.

---

26 Morgan Matzen, "'Political Football' or 'Mountain Out of a Molehill'? South Dakota Officials Clash over Indigenous Education Standards," *USA Today*, August 12, 2021, https://bit.ly/3rjzULK; Minyvonne Burke and the Associated Press, "Texas Senate Passes Bill That Removes Requirement to Teach Ku Klux Klan as 'Morally Wrong'," *NBC News*, July 21, 2021, https://nbcnews.to/376gTWB.

27 "Our Home on Native Land," Native Land Digital, October 22, 2020, https://native-land.ca.

28 "Teacher's Guide," *Native Land Digital*, October 22, 2020, https://native-land.ca/resources/teachers-guide.

To facilitate discussions and help students think critically about Indigenous history, teachers may pose the following questions while using Native Land Digital in class:

- On which tribal territories do you live?
- Which Indigenous languages are spoken in the area you live?
- On which tribal territories is the school located?
- What physical features are included in this territory?
- Why do you think Indigenous People settled in this area?
- How many territories do you see in our state?

As a formative assessment for the interactive map exercise, teachers might also consider having their students practice a Journaling activity. Journaling is the practice of recording one's thoughts, understandings, and explanations about ideas or concepts. Teachers can use this to observe how students are thinking about what they are learning. A meaningful question to explore could be, "Why is it important to acknowledge the traditional territory or ancestral lands of Indigenous People?" Allow time for free response, with no judgment. Consider encouraging students to add sketches to accompany their response.

Discussing the mistreatment of Indigenous Peoples by European colonizers and the US government can be extremely difficult for both educators and students. Teachers should prepare for these courageous conversations by seeking out current scholarly research prior to covering their lesson. Simply honoring the original people of the land on which your school is located is an excellent way to instill your students with a similar respect for all lands. When possible, consider inviting Native American citizens to visit your classroom, or maybe take a virtual field trip to the National Museum of the American Indian.[29] Continuing to seek out ways to give a voice to previously unheard perspectives helps to build empathy and understanding for your young scholars.

---

29 "Virtual Field Trips," National Museum of the American Indian, January 27, 2021, https://s.si.edu/3E6W8pC.

Ephemera: Broadsides

Ephemera is defined as items of collectible memorabilia, which are typically written or printed, and were originally expected to only have short-term usefulness or popularity. Examples include event posters, ticket stubs, political leaflets, broadsides, campaign buttons, and the like. Students are genuinely curious about unearthing items from the past, therefore, examining ephemeral collections should ignite fruitful conversations and springboard students into deep investigations of related topics.

A broadside is a sheet of paper printed on one side only. Per the Library of Congress. They were used for advertisements, political statements, public announcements, and for news events. Broadsides were intended for a limited-time use and were expected to be discarded.

However, because of their widespread publication, broadsides are the most popular ephemeral format used throughout printed history.[30] Many of these artifacts have survived and can provide viewers an insight on the daily life and public opinion of a specific region throughout history. Standards connected to historical sources and evidence, as well as causation and argumentation, can therefore be addressed using broadside analysis.

Sadly, a popular use for broadsides was employed by enslavers to advertise a reward for the return of enslaved people who sought their freedom. Using these advertisements in class can provide a powerful lesson on how enslaved people in the United States were openly and horrifically mistreated by their enslavers. Broadsides like these can be found at the National Museum of African American History and Culture's online collection and other databases provided by state historical societies, such as the Maryland Center for History and Culture and the Massachusetts Historical Society.[31]

---

30 Ibid.

31 "The Collection," National Museum of African American History and Culture, https://s. si.edu/365iUl6; "Digital Collections," Maryland Center for History and Culture, https://bit. ly/3Oi5rYH; "Collections," Massachusetts Historical Society, https://bit.ly/3KO2v3u.

To incorporate an opposing viewpoint, Digital Commonwealth hosts a large collection of abolitionist broadsides online.[32]

After locating a series of appropriate broadsides, guide students through an examination of each image with questions, such as the following:

- Who is the escaped enslaved person?
- What do we know about the enslaved person?
- Who is the enslaver?
- What do we know about the enslaver?
- Where do they live?
- When was the broadside printed?
- What was happening in the United States at this time period?

After students gather sourcing details and put the time period into context, teachers may consider having students participate in a critical thinking analysis of the broadsides using "S.I.T. and Think."

The purpose of S.I.T. and Think is to provide students with time and space to make personal observations about a primary source. I created the graphic organizer that appears in this book specifically for students to analyze broadsides; it can serve as an evidence collection tool as well as a way for students to share their personal feelings while investigating the image.

This graphic organizer could be used as a motivational strategy or as a part of the main lesson activity. Allow students three to four minutes to simply observe the image they are being asked to analyze. Next ask students to spend four to five minutes recording their observations, including these elements.

- **Interesting:** What did you find noteworthy?
- **Troubling:** What was concerning or uncomfortable?
- **Surprising:** What did you observe that you didn't expect?
- **Think:** What do you think the enslaver felt about the enslaved person who sought their freedom?

---

32 Boston Public Library, Digital Commonwealth, February 6, 2015, https://bit.ly/3uykK7s.

- How do you think the public reacted to this broadside? How did you react to it?

Create a safe space for sensitive discussions by setting ground rules with the students before you start. Ground rules may include having speakers use "I" statements to express feelings. Have classmates remain quiet and respectful to truly listen when others are speaking.

Students who are uncomfortable sharing aloud should be encouraged to share written thoughts or drawings with you. And while our classroom might be "safe," discussing this topic is never comfortable for anyone. Be mindful of that when tackling the topic of institutional slavery in America. Holding these courageous conversations with your young scholars is a step in facing the ugly truths about our nation's history and ensuring we make better decisions in how we protect the rights and freedoms for all represented in "We the People."

Unheard Perspectives Through Children's Trade Books and Graphic Novels

As shocking as this may sound, even high schoolers enjoy story time. While often overlooked for older students, children's trade books and graphic novels offer unique opportunities for students to make personal connections with otherwise overlooked historical figures or events. These types of books provide insight into emotions and personal experiences. For students who resist using traditional textbooks, trade books and graphic novels provide an excellent alternative.

With thousands of options available, teachers might partner with the school's media specialist or public librarian to seek out suitable matches to curriculum standards. Additionally, teachers might review Social Justice Booklists available from Teaching for Change.[33] A few recommended selections include:

---

33 "Booklist - Social Justice Books," SocialJusticeBooks.org, https://bit.ly/38MSLIT.

- *March* graphic novel series, by John Lewis, Andrew Aydin, and artist Nate Powell
- *The Lorax*, by Dr. Seuss
- *We Are Water Protectors*, by Carol Lindstorm
- *The Breadwinner,* by Deborah Ellis
- *The Watsons Go to Birmingham*, by Christopher Paul Curtis
- *A Long Walk to Water*, by Linda Sue Park
- *A Long Way Gone*, by Ishmael Beah
- *I Am Malala*, by Christina Lamb and Malala Yousafzai
- *The Boy Who Harnessed the Wind*, by William Kamkwamba and Bryan Mealer

These books address social emotional learning goals and increase empathy among your students. They facilitate interdisciplinary connections and provide historical perspectives. Teachers may conduct a read-aloud, a "popcorn" reading, or have their students participate in independent reading. A meaningful yet fun way to connect to the main character or event is through a Silhouette & Symbols activity—with a worksheet also created with graphic support from my son.

My purpose for creating this activity was to build empathy as well as provide an artistic assessment alternative for students. First, instruct students to brainstorm a list of facts or details about the person or event from the literature selection. Similar to the Sensory Figure activity, students will visualize their historical figure's personality, passion, and emotions tied to their respective historical events.

Ask students to think about how they could illustrate these characteristics as symbols. Teachers can provide a silhouette template for independent student work.

Conclusion

In the 1966 animated television special *It's the Great Pumpkin, Charlie Brown*, Linus warned, "There are three things I have learned never to discuss with people: religion, politics, and the Great Pumpkin."[34]

The United States has heeded Linus's advice for far too long, and it is high time we learn how to have civil discourse about highly charged topics. We know that our elementary students are capable of exercising civility, empathy, and critical thinking skills.[35] We should present students with evidence in the form of primary and secondary sources that aid their exploration into potentially controversial topics. After conducting investigations and analyzing sources, students will be able to make more accurate predictions, draw sounder conclusions, and critique past actions and events with evidence and confidence. By critically examining these sources, social studies teachers will increase student agency and maximize their engagement, making the next generation of US adults better prepared to make their own interpretations about historical and current events.

Kelly Reichardt holds a master's degree in gifted education from Johns Hopkins University and a bachelor's degree in history from the University of Maryland, Baltimore County. After teaching middle school social studies, Reichardt became a gifted and talented resource teacher. She serves as an instructional mentor to new teachers, National History Day district coordinator, and crafts social studies curriculum for Grades K–12. She was the 2017 Chamber of Commerce Outstanding Volunteer of the Year, is a 2022 National History Day Historical Argumentation scholar, and presides on the executive board for the parent association at her sons' school and scout troop.

34 *It's the Great Pumpkin, Charlie Brown*, directed by Bill Melendez (1966; Warner Home Video, 2009), DVD.

35 Catherine Gewertz, "Students Learn to Put the 'Civil' in Civil Discourse," *Education Week*, December 18, 2020, https://bit.ly/3KAqSSs; Jennifer Gunn, "Teaching Children Kindness & Empathy Using Social-Emotional Learning," ResilientEducator.com, https://bit.ly/3vcFxwH.

CHAPTER 5

"The Othering": A Conversation on Teaching on State-Sponsored Genocide

Leah Voit, St. Mary's
High School, Lancaster, New York

with Jennifer Wolfe
Oceanside High School, New York

A social studies education will vary significantly by state, district, school, and even classroom when covering critical subjects, such as state-sponsored genocides. However, even rigorous state standards may not prepare teachers for the personal and emotional challenges they face when discussing sensitive topics with their students that include genocides, war crimes, forced migrations, and other atrocities.

To better understand these challenges and how best to meet them, Leah Voit interviewed one of the most celebrated social studies teachers in her state. What follows is their dialogue on how to teach about state-sponsored genocides, including readings, resources, lesson plans, and their respective experiences and environments from opposite sides of New York State.

I grew up feeling passionate about social studies, but I never saw myself as a teacher until several part-time jobs convinced me that education was my purpose in life. I already had a communications degree from SUNY Buffalo State College, but once teaching found me, I obtained my Master of Education from Canisius College and became certified in social studies for Grades 7–12.

I began my first year as a full-time teacher at a private high school outside of Buffalo. I had my own course load, teaching New York State Regents-level global history and geography for freshmen and sophomores. It was an exciting time to become a teacher, but naturally, things changed in 2020. We shut down because of the COVID-19 pandemic and had to adapt to our new environment in major ways. As of this moment of writing, I still feel like a first-year teacher, even though it is now my third year as a COVID-era educator.

One of the most daunting tasks I face when teaching is finding ways for students to really care about the issues we discuss. For example, there are a number of state-sponsored atrocities in the past 300 years that are included in our curriculum, and they are all well-documented and consequential. I feel that teaching these sensitive topics is absolutely essential for their social studies education. As noted by Arthur W. Foshay, the former president of the Association for Supervision and Curriculum Development, a thorough understanding of history is integral to the human experience:

> The one continuing purpose of education, since ancient times, has been to bring people to as full a realization as possible of what it is to be a human being. Other statements of educational purpose have also been widely accepted: to develop the intellect, to serve social needs, to contribute to the economy, to create an effective work force, to prepare students for a job or career, to promote a particular social or political system. ... [But the] broader humanistic

purpose includes all of them, and goes beyond them, for it seeks to encompass all the dimensions of human experience.[1]

The human experience ought to be revered and cherished, particularly when preserving and passing down lessons from its failures. In social studies, I have an opportunity to show my students where we come from, where we are, and where we've yet to go. There are inspiring aspects to teaching history, but there are also topics that should weigh heavy on anybody's heart. For my students to become responsible citizens of the world, they should carry the knowledge and perspective we discuss in social studies as protection against ignorance and misinformation.

Social studies teachers throughout New York state are required to teach difficult topics—and rightfully so. I teach Global History and Geography II, which covers numerous examples of state-sponsored crimes against humanity: the Holocaust, the Armenian genocide, the Cambodian genocide, and the Rwandan genocide. The required Global I and US History courses cover similar atrocities, and our school's Participation in Government course offers students a unique opportunity for further discussion and introspection on these subjects. It is generally accepted that understanding past injustices helps ensure that we develop the empathy and capacity to prevent future wrongdoing, atrocities included. This understanding is largely why I love teaching. Optimally, I break down barriers, help students develop empathy, and make a concrete difference in society.

However, these are optimal goals. In reality, how do I accomplish these daunting tasks? How do I teach about atrocities while giving students the appropriate time they need to emotionally process them as humanitarian disasters? How do I make my students genuinely care about the past? How do I create that empathy humanity desperately begs of us to have?

---

1 Arthur W. Forshay, "The Curriculum Matrix: Transcendence and Mathematics," *Journal of Curriculum and Supervision* 6, no. 4 (Summer 1991): 277, https://bit.ly/3var1W1.

These "hows" are what keep me up at night, but they also motivate me. They keep me focused on my craft, which I always seek to improve. I am constantly reading histories alongside the pedagogy of teaching state-sponsored genocide because I understand that social studies must be taught well. Studying genocides should have an impact on a student far beyond an end-of-the-year Regents exam. It should be the sort of thing that inspires students to be more conscious, informed, and humanitarian thinkers for the rest of their lives.

As a new teacher, the personal and emotional toll of teaching students about state-sponsored genocides has often left me feeling lost, and the impacts of the COVID-19 pandemic added further weight. How do I just give a student a reading, or even a video, and guide them through such an emotionally troubling topic as if we were in person? To aid me in this professional quest, my editors on this project connected me with Jennifer Wolfe, who is a master teacher in that very subject.

Wolfe is the New York State United Teachers' 2021 Teacher of the Year. She is also a three-time Fulbright recipient, a former Social Studies Teacher of the Year, and a 25-year instructor at Long Island's Oceanside High School, a public school almost directly across the state from where I work. She had already mentored more than 20 teachers to the highest standards, so when I reached out to her for an interview, she was delighted to speak with me.[2] After Wolfe offered to share some of her experience and expertise for this essay, I transcribed our conversation and have included some of her thoughts—with minor edits—here.

I explained my personal circumstances and how I find teaching state-sponsored genocides to be a difficult task. "Mostly, I want to know what you think is your best strategy for teaching these genocides and how to thread them together," I asked.

Wolfe responded that she uses two resources almost exclusively: the Facing History and Ourselves website and Brown University's Choices Program. She added that she supplements material from

2 NYSUT Media Relations, "NYSUT Applauds Oceanside's Jennifer Wolfe as New York State's 2021 Teacher of the Year," September 14, 2020, https://bit.ly/3jwHvCI.

these sites with the "Question Formula Technique" from the Right Question Institute, and the Open Education Resources Commons.[3] All these sites provide pathways for teaching state-sponsored genocides in a responsible and engaging manner, and I recommend them as well.

> JW: What I like about the Facing History and Ourselves website is that it provides a variety of resources, such as books or lessons or videos, and they also break it down into looking at historical evidence. So if you're dealing with kids who are taking a Regents exam and they have to be able to use documents, they provide resources. If there is pushback from parents, you can say: "Look, it's a part of the curriculum as required in New York State."[4] They have a document-based question on the Regents, and you can also point to several Regents exams that have referred to genocide state-sponsored violence and have been asked about on exams. So for New York State, we're pretty protected in that it's included in the curriculum. There are requirements, and it's always on a Regents exam, either in a multiple choice or a short answer or a document.

> LV: I think that the useful part about primary sources is that it's not exactly disputable. And as teachers, we have to talk about them, especially if the Regents have the right to them.

---

3 "What is the QFT?," Right Question Institute, accessed March 15, 2022, https://bit.ly/3xuzlCG; "OER Commons," Institute for the Study of Knowledge Management in Education, accessed March 15, 2022, https://www.oercommons.org.

4 This refers to a set of required exams for New York high school students that allow them to receive a high school diploma after passing.

JW: Right, right, right. So I use Facing History and Ourselves. And because you're new, you should definitely look into their professional development. I think you'd really enjoy it. … They do week-long seminars too. For example, I did one at Bard College, and once you're in their system, they send you all kinds of other great material. What I usually do in class is I directly teach one state-sponsored genocide. I don't usually do the Holocaust even though my school is predominantly Jewish. I mean, it's a public school, but we have a lot of Jewish kids. The students have been getting the Holocaust from the time they can walk until they see me in 10th grade or 9th grade. I like to expand their view and then use the Holocaust kind of like a touchstone.

LV: My kids are predominantly Catholic. Almost exclusively.

JW: Facing History actually started out as an organization that really focused on the Holocaust and teaching about it. Now they have really expanded into other state-sponsored genocides. But also, their focus is getting kids to talk about controversial issues or about citizenship. It's a really great organization.

As promised, I found numerous readings and detailed units on state-sponsored genocides at the Facing History and Ourselves website. Their offerings on "Genocide & Mass Violence" focus primarily on the Holocaust, the Armenian Genocide, and the atrocities of Nanjing, but I also found lessons on the Rohingya crisis, the Bosnian War, and even the phenomenon of "psychic numbing."[5] The site offers resources on civic dilemmas and the events that lead to a state becoming a sponsor of violence, as well

---

5 "Genocide & Mass Violence," Facing History and Ourselves, accessed March 15, 2022, https://bit.ly/38EN7bz.

as teaching materials on other topics, including "Democracy & Civic Engagement," "Justice & Human Rights," and even "Bullying & Ostracism."[6] Each lesson plan I browsed had easy-to-read instructions that typically stated the lesson objectives, materials, warm-ups, activities, assessments, evaluations, and occasionally the amount of time that should be invested into its parts. In all, Facing History and Ourselves is indeed a valuable resource that brings students to the forefront of their lessons, which I think is particularly important when teaching topics like state-sponsored genocides.

As our conversation continued, Wolfe mentioned that she was teaching in a part of Long Island colloquially known as "Little Israel." Her students typically have a strong knowledge of antisemitism and the Holocaust before they step into her classroom, because her district covers both topics in-depth from grade school onward. She noted that Oceanside's staff included several Holocaust survivors when she started there. Learning her school's background got me thinking about where I teach and how my students do not study the Holocaust in school as regularly or as thoroughly.

I work at a co-educational suburban private Catholic high school. My students are overwhelmingly middle-class, white, and if not Catholic then usually from a Christian household with varying degrees of devotion. Since we are a standalone high school with a number of feeder schools, our students do not share a commonality to their knowledge that one might find in a unified K–12 system. Instead, my students come from different middle schools and counties throughout the Buffalo Niagara Region, and our "district" is anyone who makes it to our building. Some of our feeder schools pour many resources into a comprehensive social studies curriculum that encourages interdisciplinary learning, and some of their teachers might even offer an in-depth lesson on the Holocaust.

The remaining schools merely follow their state mandated social studies requirements. So, to generalize, most of my new students have a superficial understanding of the Holocaust.

6 "Topics," Facing History and Ourselves, accessed March 15, 2022, https://www.facinghistory.org/topics.

These circumstances factored into why I found the Facing History and Ourselves website particularly helpful. The lessons in their unit on the Armenian Genocide touched on the historical facts of the atrocity as well as the American response to it. This latter detail is important because it brings the subject closer to home for my students.[7]

However, Facing History and Ourselves goes a step further. Their "Identity and Belonging" lesson asks students to create "two identity charts, one for themselves and one for Arshile Gorky," an American artist and refugee from the Armenian Genocide.[8] By having the students compare their identities alongside Gorky's, the exercise connects with students on a personal level. The assessment then has teachers ask their students, "What event or events from the past have influenced my identity?"[9] Such an existential exercise will likely stay with students after they leave the classroom in ways that all educators should strive for.

Wolfe added that, in her classroom, students make personal assessments while considering aspects of official government policy.

> **JW:** In my AP human geography class, where I have 11th and 12th graders, we do a whole unit on political violence against different races and different ethnicities. We also ask the question, "How should the US respond to genocide?"

> **LV:** Oh, that is a really interesting unit.

---

7 "Crimes Against Humanity and Civilization: The Genocide of the Armenians," Facing History and Ourselves, accessed March 15, 2022, https://bit.ly/37byBb3; "American Responses to the Armenian Genocide," Facing History and Ourselves, accessed March 15, 2022, https://bit.ly/3uzHvIg.

8 "Identity and Belonging," Facing History and Ourselves, accessed March 15, 2022, https://bit.ly/3NZTl6h.

9 Ibid.

JW: That unit actually comes from the Choices Program from Brown University. And they talk about how you have to remember that in all of these units, no matter who you're using or if you're creating it yourself, you have to start with the vocabulary. The kids need to actually know what it means to say "genocide," and they need to know the definitions. And they should always start with some required reading, something that they all have to read together so that they all have the same facts. I think that's really important.

There are several things to appreciate in Wolfe's approach to this subject. Her unit on political violence makes an excellent companion to the "Identity and Belonging" lesson mentioned earlier. While fine separately, these two lessons together could let students apply everything they learned about self and empathy to those around them when discussing genocide, political violence, and other hot button topics. Asking how US leaders should respond to genocides is also an excellent exercise. Each student's morals and perspectives can contribute to discussions, and it is possible that their conclusions would not be dissimilar from actual enacted US policy. In brief, these exercises could transform any classroom into a facsimile of the White House Situation Room, and any participating student into our nation's youngest president!

The Choices Program that Wolfe mentioned centers around finding "the point" of a lesson beyond passing an exam or completing an exercise. Although I love social studies, I can't expect each student to want to read primary sources. Studying difficult or traumatic history might feel daunting for some, especially if there is the classic burning question in the back of their minds, "What is the point of this?"

The Choices Program has readings, lessons, and videos for teachers to better connect past events with modern public policy in the United States.[10] Their readings offer the common starting points that Wolfe suggested, namely by compiling materials that include primary sources as a baseline of knowledge for students. And while a Choices Program curriculum unit would be purchased by a teacher's individual school, the free videos are great starting points. For example, one video asks and expertly answers in the span of just two minutes, "Why Should High School Students Learn About Human Rights?"[11] That is a critical question for anyone teaching about a state-sponsored genocide and the said state's role in violating those rights.

Because teaching about genocide is inherently sensitive and traumatic material, Wolfe advises against doing slideshow presentations or navigating photo galleries in lieu of readings and discussions.

> **LV:** There's a reverence that you need. I think activities like that are lacking. It's why we're teaching.
>
> **JW:** Yes. And also, what's the point of doing it that way? I mean, if you're answering a larger essential question and you're asking kids to look at genocide as the data for answering the question, then that makes sense to me. So if you're talking about the impact, let's say, of World War I on Europe, and [you] want to focus on the historical theme of social or cultural impact, … now we can talk about the Holocaust in light of that lens. So that they can see—
>
> **LV:** Okay, why is that? Why do we have that structure?

10 "Inside a Choices Curriculum Unit," The Choices Program, January 16, 2020, accessed March 15, 2022, https://bit.ly/3M2wNQf.

11 Tanya Monforte, "Why Should High School Students Learn About Human Rights?," The Choices Program, filmed May 28, 2009, video, 2:22, https://bit.ly/3rosK99.

JW: Well, because then [the students] are like, "Oh, look at all these economic issues and these political issues." They get all the conditions first, right? You contextualize the Holocaust for them. So then when they see it happening, they're like, "Oh, it makes sense. They're looking for somebody to blame. These people were seemingly different from everybody else."

LV: Right. I've always wanted to say this is such a human thing that we're all vulnerable to. Monsters don't do these things. People do them.

JW: Right, exactly.

LV: And government systems.

JW: Exactly. Yes, right. Even now we're still seeing these state-sponsored genocides from Rwanda to South Sudan. And in this country, certainly after 9/11, there was a lot of public fervor around Muslims. Of course, the government didn't go around encamping them, but we did do that to the Japanese during World War II. So, a larger question might be, "What are the conditions for state-sponsored genocide? What are the conditions that create the harsh treatment of the 'other'?"[12]

LV: Like why the other people? Why do we other them?

JW: [We] can approach this topic from lots of different ways, right? You can approach it from the history and the impact of World War I on Europe, or you can

---

12 Two excellent online resources on "othering" can be found at: Clint Curle, "Us vs. Them: The Process of Othering," Canadian Museum for Human Rights, accessed March 15, 2022, https://bit.ly/37eBc3Z; and "The Process of Othering," Montreal Holocaust Museum, accessed March 15, 2022, https://bit.ly/3xuzlCG.

approach it as a "universe of obligation" question. Like, if you have a class ... where you're asking, "Who are we responsible for? What does it mean to be an American?" And then you can take a look at times in history when the US has othered other people. They include Native Americans, African Americans, the Japanese during WWII, and Muslims after 9/11. You can also take a look at how the state has sponsored these kinds of separations, and why. And looking at the impact of those separations, their social impact, their economic impact, their political impact, that gives you cover, frankly. So that it's clear that you're not saying: "Oh, the white people are terrible, look what they've done." No, you were talking about it in terms of policy decisions that were created by particular conditions in society at that time, and then this is what happened.

This public aspect to genocide is where I find the material can feel daunting at times. I want my students to understand that state-sponsored genocides begin and end with decisions made by ordinary people. But this is a nuanced point, and I must be careful when approaching it in class. It would be irresponsible to go before my students and tell them, "Under certain circumstances, some of you might enable genocide." It is not a responsible or realistic thing to say, and it would be immediately upsetting to my students and their parents.

What I *can* do is show students how everything adds up. I can present the humanity of even the bad actors, because when an entire state is engaging in an awful action, individuals can be led to appalling choices. Adolf Hitler and Pol Pot were not supernatural monsters. They were human beings, but both men were directly responsible for especially monstrous acts. However, they were not solely responsible for their respective crimes against humanity. They needed allies, subordinates, and followers to help them consolidate power, eliminate rivals, and ultimately put their worst plans into action. "Ordinary" people contributed to these genocides, and that is something that every ordinary person should know.

As for the leaders of genocide, in my opinion, the "Great Man Theory" of history is best disproven by Herbert Spencer in his 1860 book *The Study of Sociology*:

> You must admit that the genesis of a great man depends on the long series of complex influences which has produced the race in which he appears, and the social state into which that race has slowly grown. ... Before he can remake his society, his society must make him.[13]

To call these individuals "great men" is an affront to historical study. State-sponsored genocides have happened throughout history. They continue happening and most likely will happen again. The current genocide of the Rohingya people in Myanmar or the extermination of Uyghurs in China are particularly important for students to know about. They are happening right now.

The critical thinking lessons we use in social studies classrooms can be excellent ways to protect against such prejudice while simultaneously educating students. The exercises can function like a drill in sports practice, or an etude for a musician: something for young minds to commit to memory and process almost unconsciously. My conversation with Wolfe continued on this subject:

> **JW:** You can ask, "How has the United States responded to state-sponsored genocides?" And students can start to think about the United States' role in the Armenian genocide, or the Holocaust, or the Cambodian genocide, or Bosnia, or Rwanda, or other examples. How you deal with genocide really depends on the class that you're teaching, whether

---

13 Herbert Spencer, The Study of Sociology (London: Appleton, 1896), 15, as quoted in Peter E. Gordon and Warren Breckman, eds., *The Cambridge History of Modern European Thought: Volume II, The Twentieth Century* (Cambridge: Cambridge University Press, 2019), 26.

they're ninth graders or sixth graders or 11th graders. It's a very different lesson for different ages, and a very different focus depending on the group. You have to consider, what larger issue do I really want them to understand about this?

What you really want, I'm assuming, is to teach them how we can learn from these past mistakes and then how we don't do that again. Of particular importance is having the students recognize conditions that can lead to these travesties. The key is that there are conversations you can have with kids if you've built a decent relationship with them. And there are conversations you can have with students if they're older. Kids will let you teach them very sensitive topics as long as you have done the work before of building relationships with them.

There is always a way to illuminate the issue. For example, [using] the Board of Education hoopla [referring to outrage expressed prior to the 2021–2022 school year about mask mandates in schools] when a kid asks me, "How could the Holocaust possibly have happened in Germany? Germans just stood by."

My thought in response is, let's pull the tape from the Board of Education meeting where people were basically fighting to be able to infect their neighbors with COVID because they didn't want to wear a mask. I mean, it happened. Look, after a period of economic depression when [unemployment rose and people were not leaving their homes], some citizens thought the government was manhandling everyone. To those people who were so inclined, geez, maybe they really did think it looked like Nazi Germany in 1937.[14]

14 See also "Godwin's law," named for US attorney Mike Godwin: "As an online discussion continues, the probability of a reference or comparison to Hitler or Nazis approaches 1." "I Seem to Be a Verb," *Jewcy*, April 30, 2008, https://bit.ly/3uECEWG.

LV: Those student relationships are the hugest thing.

JW: It is, you can't teach the sensitive information, whether it's state-sponsored genocide or the elections, you can't teach any of that sensitive information unless you have made a relationship with those kids.

LV: That's what I struggled with last year [2020–2021]. Because everything was [remote, I felt like] I didn't know my kids. They were on the computer. Those conversations where I am getting to know people and taking an interest in their lives didn't happen.

JW: … It was tough. And the thing is, I mean on a good day, you have to have a relationship with your students and to get them to work in a normal setting. …

LV: Right. Yeah, it was crazy.

JW: But [as to] genocide, the Choices Program is great from Brown. It's about 18, 16 or 18 pages and it's all handouts and readings and case studies. And again, case studies are great as long as you have an overarching question that they're supposed to be looking at these case studies to find the answer for it. It can't just be about the act of genocide. There are so many factors. And of course, for teachers, are we [merely] teaching how bad people can be to one another? I'm not really sure what the point of that is, you know what I mean? We want it to be about so much more …

And the other thing I love to use when I'm doing difficult topics is the Question Formulation Technique … from the Right Question Institute … and they have free templates on their website for people who want to use them and all you have to do is plug in a prompt and then just follow along in the slide deck.

I should note that the Right Question Institute is a free resource that focuses on asking intuitive, relatable questions. Their Question Formulation Technique (QFT) is a way to dig into the why of a question, and it engages students in further inquiry.[15] I found this particularly useful since one of the focuses of my graduate studies involved asking engaging questions that spiral into higher order thinking and learning. Another goal was for us to be as student-centered as possible. The QFT template links these two objectives in ways that I am confident other educators will find helpful.

The type of lesson that Wolfe described is excellent for building relationships with students centered on their own specific learning.

JW: … what's great is that the prompt could be an essential question or maybe a photograph or a reading or a video clip … whatever you want to be. And then the kids … come up with as many questions as they can in approximately the next four minutes about the prompt. Then they go back and make all of their closed-ended questions into open-ended questions. And so you show them how to do that.

Next, I get them to sit in pairs. Let's say everybody had 10 or 15 questions. I tell each pair that I want

15 "What is the QFT?" Right Question Institute, accessed March 15, 2022, from https:// rightquestion.org/what-is-the-qft/.

them to pick the top five questions between the two of them … and then each pair of students joins another pair. In that group of four, you've now got 10 really good questions. Again, I direct them to narrow their questions down to five really good questions. So even with a small class, now you've got 20 to 25 questions that the class is really interested in having answered.

I say to the students, "These are the questions that we want to focus on. Let's figure out what we want to do with those questions. Do you want to create a slide deck? Do you want to do a podcast? Do you want to do some interviews? Do you want to write an article for the school newspaper?" The real question is, how do they want their learning to be produced? This gives the students a choice. So, their project is now geared to their overarching questions that they themselves want to know the answers to, and they are producing something to illustrate the learning that they want to do.

At this point, your job is to make sure they have the information and evidence and document resources to do that work. You facilitate what they're doing in each of the groups. What I have found is sometimes the groups will all have the same problem with a particular thing or particular understanding. Then you can stop and do a mini-lesson for 10 to 15 minutes. For example, "Let's take a look at a comparative timeline and let's look at all the causes of all these genocides. Is there something that is the same?" And you can take some time and do some direct teaching in between their project work.

LV: This is a really cool experience in the classroom. It sounds like everything that you want in a lesson.

JW: Absolutely. And that way they create whatever they want and then you say, "Okay, would you like us to look at this just in the class? Would you like to share your work with other people?" When projects are done, we've published [them] on Google Sites or even attached projects to the school website if it's excellent and the administration agrees. We do all kinds of things like that.

My own school is trying to develop additional opportunities for students to do more meaningful, outward-facing work. Published projects offer students a chance to be proud of their academic achievements beyond their intrinsic value. Our goal in the next year or so is to highlight student work regularly through our email newsletter and to link to such efforts on social media. For young people in my class, the message has essentially been, "All right, you have learned and grown to care about this topic, and now we are going to share that learning with others. Your work may make a difference in someone else's life."

Naturally, there will always be challenges, which Wolfe and I discussed:

LV: [Is there] anything that you do for any student who's being particularly difficult throughout?

JW: I let them be difficult. ... We just had this conversation this morning ... "Well, how can I know if it's the truth?" I tell them that we are all entitled to our own opinions, but we are not entitled to our own facts. So ... I tell them, "Listen, I'm not telling you what you can and cannot think. I'm giving you, and you're finding, the actual primary source documents from these events ... and looking at these documents. What do you think about them?"

And then if you have a particular kid who is a neo-Nazi … In my school, most of the kids in the class will handle the kid themselves. They usually shut them down [so to speak.] … Our other mantra in our classes is that we're tough on ideas, but we're soft on people. So what they will do is attack the kids' ideas and bring up laws that exist … so that [a reactionary student] is constantly being answered with facts.

LV: I love that.

JW: But I do not ever tell them to not be able to say what they want. That is the beginning of an argument for you that you don't want to deal with, you know what I mean?

LV: Yeah, you can't win it.

When teaching about state-sponsored genocide, there will almost always be students who will take things at least one step too far. Sometimes these young people seek shock value and attention, and other times they genuinely have a problematic belief. Students who fall into either category can incite what I never show but will disclose within this essay as a panic in my soul, but neither the attention seekers nor the problematic students are impossible to deal with. As mentioned, they will always be in social studies classrooms. It comes with the job.

Thankfully, my experience with attention seekers is largely the same as Wolfe's: Other students see right through the problematic behavior. The key is to establish the classroom environment ahead of time, which Wolfe detailed later in our conversation. If the learning environment promotes healthy discourse and students are unafraid to speak, then the shock value of what this type of student says carries much less weight. Their provocation will eventually fizzle out.

When studying genocide myself, it became apparent that while pseudoscientific beliefs are largely debunked, they still leak into our modern conversations. Phrenology, physical anthropometry, and polygenism all are examples of these types of theories. I take comfort in the fact that such "race science" has been repeatedly discredited. When a student suggests a problematic theory, myth, or worldview, my job as a teacher is to guide them to understanding. But the fact is that verbal battles with students are tough.

> JW: ... you can't win them all. What you can do is show students ... the facts and the sources that you have to use [so] they're not on neo-Nazi sources or QAnon sites. They're using your resources. ... [The] best resources are from the Library of Congress or the UN, or other credible organizations that they can't undermine. ...
> Make sure that you have created space in your lesson planning beforehand so that even before this student starts, they understand how to [do what the Open Educational Resource (OER) Project] calls a "claim test."[16] The purpose is so that students... become more skillful in evaluating others' claims so that they really learn to be critical consumers of the news, of media, of information.

> JW: [Claim testing] helps give a basic understanding [of] the questions, "How do we decide what to believe? How do we know what we know?" [The students] find out that there's actually a way to test claims and a way to find out if what people are saying is true, etc. But that work has to happen before you

16 The Open Educational Resource (OER) Project is a free educational resource that offers plenty of materials for teachers to use. It started as one course called "Big History," that stems from David Christian's "The History of Our World in 18 Minutes," March 2011, video, https://bit.ly/3vgqcuQ. For more information on the OER Project, see "Frequently Asked Questions," OER Project, accessed March 15, 2022, https://bit.ly/3JCl5KJ.

do the work of a genocide unit. I would never do a genocide unit in the first 10 weeks of school.

LV: Yeah. That makes sense.

JW: Because that is a unit that requires that you have built an atmosphere of learning where the kids feel respected, you feel respected, they understand where you're coming from, things like that. ... You can't just hop into this.

LV: Right. ... having a classroom environment is probably the biggest thing.

JW: Yeah. I mean, knowing your students and then creating a classroom with respect and excitement about learning is really essential. If you don't do that, you can't do these things.

LV: It's not going to go well if you try.

JW: ... It's not going to go well is right, yeah.

What I find particularly compelling about the OER Project is the way it teaches the intersection of science and history. What has stood out to me is how we teach our subjects as separate disciplines: math is math, science is science, English is English, etc. In reality, everything intersects, and some of the greatest discoveries in history involved connecting previously unrelated fields. Much of the history that we study in my class exists because of the science my students study, and we study it using specific languages that have evolved with time and place. The OER Project offers students a way to connect disciplines and provides another "point" to learning. Its "claims test" provides a way for social studies teachers to arrive at conclusions and understanding in a logical way in their classrooms.

Historically, we find that when a state's leaders aim to conduct a genocide, many of their claims typically go untested. If they are tested, the state might verify its own claims with bad science, such as phrenology or physical anthropometry. For example, leaders of Nazi Germany promoted the "Aryans" as a genetically superior race, going so far as to exterminate anyone who did not conform to Aryan appearance. Through claims testing, students would become intellectually able to debunk these sorts of assertions on their own.

Student relationships and classroom management are critical to the ability to teach any controversial topics, let alone teaching state-sponsored genocides. For learning to take place, students need to feel comfortable, especially when the material can be shocking or disturbing.

> **JW:** Any controversial topic requires at least 10 weeks of teaching them who you are, learning who they are, and setting up your norms and practices in your room. We spend at least three or four days on norm setting. We write those norms out on big red paper, and they are posted around the room. And when there's an issue, I point, and I go, "This is the one you liked, you picked this norm, what are we doing?" That is not wasted time. ... [N]orming your classroom must be done. ... Brené Brown, I think, has students decide what things are important to them, what values, and then she has them say, "Okay, what does that value look like in our classroom?"
>
> And then we take everyone's answers and the students pick the top five or six of them that they really identify with and think are necessary for a productive classroom. And that's kind of nice. ... Their rules are based on what they value, [and that is important] because most of the time, students are told what they will do, you know what I mean? Or even what they value.

This norm-setting Ms. Wolfe describes is linked with her students' understanding of how a government can conduct a genocide. When a genocide is carried out it is because the norms allow it. For Nazi Germany, anti-Semitism was the norm. For Cambodians, discontent with the previous leadership was the norm. These norms allowed for actions that we find shocking to be less alarming in the moment.

My second year of teaching yielded one of my most memorable moments. My class was analyzing excerpts from Hitler's *Mein Kampf*. We did so with guiding questions to try to understand who the man was and how he became what he did. After reading one of the excerpts, a student shook his head and demanded, "How did these people not know?!" The conversation that followed led to genuine engaged learning and discussion and sparked the involvement in the entire unit. Not only did our classroom norms allow this student to offer his thoughts, but the norms also led us to inquire into sensitive history itself.

Learning history is a journey that a classroom takes together. Just to reiterate the point, there needs to be a level of comfort with the classroom so that when atrocities are introduced, we are able to take a deep dive into the historical how and why. While I am on the topic of productive learning environments, Wolfe certainly afforded me one. What follows is the end of our conversation.

> LV: My last question for you is, Do you have any [further] lasting advice … for a younger, newer teacher?

> JW: I would say to go online and search for the book *What Teachers Should Know and Be Able to Do*.[17] There's a free PDF [of it]. [I]t comes from the National Board for Professional Teaching Standards, and it outlines the five core propositions of what we do in our rooms every day and [a younger, newer teacher] should

17 National Board for Professional Teaching Standards, *What Teachers Should Know and Be Able to Do* (Arlington, VA: National Board for Professional Teaching Standards, 2016), retrieved from https://bit.ly/3EaGR7o.

read it. I think it's 50 pages. And what's nice about it is it lays out exactly the complexities of our work: ... the importance of learning who your students are, and learning your subject, and how to teach those subjects to students, that you are responsible for managing and monitoring student learning, that you think systematically about your practice and you learn from this experience. And then lastly, that you are a member of a learning community.

The five core propositions are detailed, giving examples that show a new teacher what they look like in the room. I find that's a very concise, well-researched piece by a well-respected organization. It has a program that gives teachers the profession's highest certification from. It's like being a board-certified doctor or a board-certified accountant. In this case, it's being a board-certified teacher[,] and this is the organization that runs that program. I think when you are brand new, you get a lot of advice from a lot of different people. ... I think reading that book and going with your gut, as long as your gut is pointed at your students and what they need, you can't really go wrong ... because you're the only one in the room with those kids. I mean, veteran teachers can give you tips and tricks for sure, absolutely, and they can help you puzzle things out and that is definitely true. But you are in the room with the kids, and you get to know them, and you have to trust your gut that you know what they need. And then to meet those needs, you figure that out by reading that little book and by talking to other people in your school.

LV: Thank you.

JW: You're welcome.

My conversation with Wolfe was absolutely what I needed to hear as I navigate my own career. Being a new teacher in an ever-evolving landscape with material I find difficult is a weighty responsibility, but as I gather expertise and confidence, I feel a lot of it comes down to trusting myself.

Teaching about a subject as sensitive as state-sponsored genocides can feel "iffy" in today's political climate, but that is all the more reason to teach it. This subject goes far beyond the facts of history: My hope is that learning about past injustices offers us a chance to teach humanity and develop empathy and understanding to build toward a better world. Of course, in order to develop empathy and understanding, I need to possess those traits myself. I also need to train myself in pedagogy well beyond the minimum required, but the resources Wolfe suggested are a phenomenal start.

Leah Voit is a social studies teacher at St. Mary's High School in Lancaster, New York. Her classes include Global History and Geography II, and she coaches her school's junior varsity soccer team. Voit is a determined and effective communicator with a passion for performance, the fine arts, and sports. She is also an experienced dancer, choreographer, and designer.

Jennifer Wolfe, 2021 New York State Teacher of the Year, has been teaching social studies at Oceanside High School for 25 years. She is a National Board Certified Teacher in AYA Social Studies, the recipient of three Fulbright Scholarships, winner of the National Education Association Foundation 2022 California Casualty Teaching Excellence Award, a published author, speaker, mom, and an unapologetic proponent of teacher leadership. Wolfe wholeheartedly believes that the challenges we face today in education can best be solved with a table full of teachers leading the way. She currently teaches Pre-AP World History, AP Human Geography, and Participation in Government.

CHAPTER 6

Shared Perspectives: Empowering Classroom Communities for Important Conversations

Brooke Brown
Washington High School, Washington

with Kim Bond, Paul Cavanagh, Chance Las Dulce, Julien Pollard, and Matt Price

For this final chapter, educator Brooke Brown presents something akin to a panel discussion. She provided an opportunity for different educators to connect and share their experiences teaching social studies, and then organized their experiences into a single essay. What follows is an ambitious examination of education with regard to community, diversity, inclusion, and interconnectedness. Each contributors' section begins with their name.

We thank everyone who contributed to Brown's ambitious examination of community, diversity, and interconnectedness in education.

Chance Las Dulce

I have been an educator for the past seven years at the elementary, middle, and high school levels. I am currently teaching high school English and Ethnic Studies in Tacoma, Washington. I identify as a multiracial man, and I passionately help my students discover who they are so that they can better understand the world around them.

The most important component to the foundation of a classroom is an authentic and caring relationship with our students. To establish this, we need to re-imagine our classrooms and educational spaces. One way of doing this is by decolonizing our educational system, which means shifting from hierarchical power structures to one more focused on community.

At the start of the school year, one of my first activities with my students is to construct agreements that reinforce the community we're building in our classroom. I present a guiding principle known as In Lak'ech, a neo-Mayan moral concept most famously described by Chicano playwright Luis Valdez as meaning, "You are my other me."[1] The expression communicates the interconnectedness between people in our community and across the world, and its foundational belief is that our successes and survival are contingent on each other.[2]

This concept reflects the community I hope to see in our educational spaces: one that communicates our interconnectedness and where we view each other as a whole. In our society and schools, we are often trained and even indoctrinated to focus on ourselves as individuals. It is an egocentric outlook, which is undesirable and even destructive in a diverse and shared environment. When we view ourselves as a community of students, educators, administrators, families, and other people, it forces us to change perspectives to one more befitting empathy and mutual respect. The latter environment is far better suited for difficult conversations since it requires us to understand that each opinion

---

1 Jorge Huerta, introduction to Luis Valdez, *Zoot Suit and Other Plays* (Houston: Arte Publico Press, 1992), 10.

2 Brian W. McNeill and Joseph M. Cervantes, eds., Latina/o Healing Practices: Mestizo and Indigenous Perspectives (New York: Routledge, 2008), 13; Javier Calvo de Mora and Kerry J. Kennedy, eds., *Schools and Informal Learning in a Knowledge-Based World* (New York: Routledge, 2020), 123.

of the subjects we discuss affects us all. In Lak'ech helps students see the benefits of such an altruistic learning environment while empowering them to resist the many covert signals and messages seeking to divide them.

After a discussion of In Lak'ech, I give students full autonomy to decide how we want our classroom to function and what our norms should be. I ask them to agree on these in groups before we talk through them as a class. (As an aside, using groups is another strategy for building community and fostering collaboration rather than individual seating arrangements or independent work.)

As we talk about what each group has come up with, I employ another decolonial teaching tactic. We have been trained to believe that democratic structures of decision making are what is "fair." However, a decision that 49 percent of a group favors and 51 percent opposes is not serving the needs of everyone. In Indigenous communities, the decisions are made by consensus, meaning everyone comes to an agreement. I use this same model when I teach. As a community, we must come to an accord about how our class will function. Community agreements will only work as intended if everyone participates in it, not just a majority. An all-inclusive process deconstructs the traditional power system of our educational spaces by giving students complete control over how their class should operate. It also teaches students how to care for one another in a community. It ensures that everyone's voice is heard and valued.

Another way that educators can facilitate difficult conversations is to create environments where such discourse is commonplace. I think that part of the reason these conversations are even considered "difficult" is because they are not held in schools as frequently as they should be, which deprives both students and educators of valuable experience in them. So many experiences and injustices have either been diluted or erased to preserve the spurious "master narrative" that those in power throughout US history got there through hard work. To fight against this message of white supremacy and Manifest Destiny, we need to center Black, Indigenous, and People of Color (BIPOC) voices in our classrooms.

This means not only amplifying the voices of our BIPOC students, but also making sure that they see themselves in our curriculum. In my classes, nearly every text that we read is by a BIPOC author. This accomplishes two things. First, it exposes students to the histories, narratives, and perspectives of BIPOC voices and other marginalized groups and identities. Second, because of this exposure, it's not disorienting when my students have discussions on their readings. It's what they've always done.

My students know they will discuss difficult topics at length in my classroom, and together, we learn not to shy from them. I believe that if more teachers commit to featuring marginalized voices, it will create rich opportunities for our students to facilitate the kinds of meaningful conversations that students want and need to have.

Matt Price (he/him)

I am in my seventh year as an educator at the high school level. I currently teach Environmental Science and Food Justice in Tacoma, Washington, on the land of the spuyaləpabš (the Puyallup Nation) and the Coast Salish Peoples. I identify as a white man, and am working toward being an ally and co-conspirator for justice and liberation with my students and community.

I am a science educator. For me, the key to having difficult conversations with students is to normalize these discussions in your learning community. By using our content to focus on our students' identities, issues, and challenges, we can support a classroom culture where challenging topics can be discussed. Like any other skill, conversations that highlight systemic oppression and inequity take practice.[3] If students only have sporadic opportunities to engage in these conversations, they will never develop the comfort or ability to move into a space where trauma can be addressed and healing can occur.

---

3 Namely, discrimination arising from established social and cultural structures and expectations.

We might treat these difficult discussion topics as separate from our "classroom content." And to be sure, conversations on systemic racism and other oppressions merit extra care. Where many "content based" classroom discussions and arguments are based on facts/data, process, or purpose, conversations around race can be intensely personal as a key piece of our cultural and individual identity.[4] Opening the opportunity but "otherizing" the conversation sends students a signal that this topic is disconnected from our experiences and learning in the classroom.

As an example, during the Standing Rock Sioux protests and actions against the Dakota Access Pipeline in 2016, I created a "special time" during the beginning of each class to update, converse, and share about what we were collectively witnessing. My classes engaged in conversations on race, Indigenous rights, and the history of land theft. However, these conversations were uncomfortable, and lacked the rigor and vigor I expected. By establishing a clear separation from our "normal" content, I unwittingly gave these conversations less value in the eyes of my students. I have a distinct memory of a student asking, "I don't understand why these people are getting treated so badly. But what does this have to do with environmental science?"

Of course, my brain was spinning, seeing the countless connections between race, land use and land theft, Indigenous history, water ecology, and Indigenous scientific epistemology. Why couldn't my students see these connections? I had failed to normalize these conversations from day one of my class. I had also failed to prepare students with the critical analysis to connect the Western scientific understanding of water ecology and habitat fragmentation with the culmination of systemic injustices we were seeing unfold daily. Looking back, I see this was a missed opportunity to integrate my curriculum fully around the Standing Rock protests. I should have been creating class-long opportunities to engage in the scientific dialogue and critically interrogate the connection between our shared history and systemic injustice—

4 Matthew R. Kay, *Not Light, But Fire: How to Lead Meaningful Race Conversations in the Classroom* (Portsmouth, NH: Stenhouse Publishers, 2018) 39–61.

rather than relying on a 10-minute current events conversation before we returned to our regular programming.

I recognize how difficult it can feel to find connections to systemic issues in our content areas. When I am planning, I am asking myself, Is there an opportunity to bring in conversations about race into my content? As an example: During my soil science unit, we learn about why living soils are foundational to all life. On paper, this content is limited to ultra-nerd level microscope-wielding Western science, and we could leave it there. However, this is an incredible opportunity to explore how access to living soil to grow food is a crucial piece of food sovereignty for Black, Indigenous, and communities of color, and how that access has been systematically denied throughout American history. Black farmers are currently just 1.4 percent of the US farming population.[5]

The anchoring question for the soil science unit becomes, Why is living soil so crucial for BIPOC food sovereignty? We must now learn the science and the historical context that has led to the denial of land access. To do this we need to understand racist policies, such as convict leasing, sharecropping, theft of Indigenous land and land owned by BIPOC farmers, and more. Additionally, this becomes an opportunity to center BIPOC. They include Fannie Lou Hamer and the Freedom Farm, Booker T. Whatley, a founder of organic agriculture, and George Washington Carver, the first Black man to get an agricultural science degree and also a foundational figure in restorative soil science. Going further back, I can reference Indigenous and Afro-Indigenous soil management techniques, such as Terra Preta from the Amazon Region.

Normalizing the connection between scientific knowledge, theory, and practice with the critical analysis of the systems in our society has shifted the dynamic in my classroom. Conversations about race, racism, and systems of oppression are part of our daily dialogue and as important to our understanding of the content as the science itself. I also agree with my colleagues that creating a space to address and discuss systemic issues daily in your classroom

---

5 US Department of Agriculture, "2017 Census of Agriculture Highlights: Black Producers," ACH17-9, October 2019, https://bit.ly/37bzIrf.

helps students develop the comfort, language, and skills to explore these ideas.[6]

It is a challenge to find a balance between facilitating class conversations versus being an active participant. As educators, we are trained to be neutral parties. This can support critical thinking in our students, yet neutrally facilitating conversations around identity can do harm to BIPOC students. As a white male educator, I have incredible power in the classroom. To shift power to my students, I cannot be a neutral party in these conversations. I am always ready to step in from a place of love and empathy if a discussion moves toward perpetuating oppressive ideas. After all, there are no two sides of an argument when dialogue turns to talking about the relative humanity of our different communities or the rights of our students to exist.

As an example, what follows is a conversation that touched on the Agricultural H2-A Visa program and undocumented workers in agriculture. After clarifying the issues, I am able to move the conversation in a direction to help students build a collective purpose for justice.

> **Student A:** Wait, so there is a legal way to be a farmworker here? Why would people come work here illegally?
>
> **Student B:** Yo, no one is illegal, people are just trying to survive.
>
> **Student A:** Yeah, but they can go through the system, it seems way smarter.
>
> **Studen B:** Who are you calling dumb, dude?
>
> **Mr. P:** All right, Student A. Can I ask you a clarifying question?
>
> **Student A:** Sure.
>
> **Mr. P:** What I'm hearing you say, is that you don't understand why people would choose to cross the border for what we now know is often an even poorer working experience?

---

6 Kay, *Not Light, But Fire*, 14–38.

Student A: Yeah, exactly.

Mr. P: So that makes sense to me, but I'm also hearing you connect the intelligence of a group of people with that decision. When you are using the word "they" like that, the impact on me is you are lumping a group of people together, and it doesn't feel respectful. I mean, can you even imagine having to make that decision? It's definitely not my lived experience. We know firsthand how hard this work can be.

Student A: Yeah, I guess not.

Mr. P: All right, so let's tell this story again: What are some of the factors we have discussed that have created this system in the first place, whether that is H2A or undocumented workers feeding us?

Student B: Our need for lots of affordable labor, NAFTA.

Mr. P: Keeping going, help them out.

Other Student: Perpetuation of the plantation agriculture model?

Mr. P: For sure—and who has the power in this relationship—do these farm workers have a lot of power?

Student A: Hell no, The food companies, the government.

Mr. P: Okay, so Student A, you told us initially you thought more people should be going through the H2A program, so how would you change that system to make access easier?

Student A: Um … Probably pay people more? Maybe make sure all the stuff is in a language people that want to work can read.

Mr. P: Now we are getting somewhere. We've got to stay focused on the systems in power that can make those changes

Student A: Yeah, my bad Student B.

Kim Bond

I have worked in education for seven years and have spent the past three as a classroom teacher at the middle level. I currently teach eighth-grade English language arts in Parkland, Washington. I identify as a queer, multiracial woman who is passionate about providing students with a space where they can be wholly and authentically themselves.

Genuine relationship building is the most important thing that any teacher can invest their time on. Yes, even more important than the curriculum. I believe that if we are unsuccessful in meeting our students with care and compassion, then there is no way for us to even think about entering into challenging or sensitive classroom conversations.

When considering how to best prepare our students and the classroom environment for difficult conversations, I think of immediately building relationships with them centered in student agency. This may sound obvious, like I have set myself up with a "gimme" question to answer.[7] But when I speak with my students about teachers who they struggle with, the students feel those teachers do not listen to them, nor care about what the students have to share. In short, their relationship has failed.

To start off the year, I put the desks in groups and have the students choose their own seats. I find that starting the school year that way demonstrates to my students that they can make their own choices in the classroom, and that their voices impact the decisions that I make as their teacher. I know some teachers may feel this lacks structure for the beginning of the year, or for a way to run a classroom year-round. However, I believe we should do what works best for our students, rather than what works best for us as educators.

I routinely ask students what they require, which I gauge through surveys, one-on-one conversations, group discussions, and writing prompts. This approach is designed to show my students that their voices matter. If they have an issue with something,

---

7 That is, an easy question.

especially if it is related to their education, they need to advocate for themselves. It is an important lesson. It is hard to heal something if you cannot first identify the wound. For many of our students, a great way to begin healing from their experiences with the US education system—because it is a system that has historically forcefully assimilated students into the dominant culture, language, and traditions—is by being provided the opportunity to be their whole authentic selves in our schools.[8]

To reinforce that opportunity, I supplement the district curriculum with resources that reflect my students. Most of my students are people of color, but many curricular resources fail to provide multiple perspectives, or to include material from BIPOC writers. So I seek out resources that were created by historically marginalized communities.[9] Most of these resources are books that we read part of together. Some of the books include *Long Way Down* by Jason Reynolds; *Crown: An Ode to the Fresh Cut* by Derrick Barnes and Gordon C. James; *Furia* by Yamile Saied Mendez; *Other Words for Home* by Jasmine Warga; and *Living Beyond Borders: Growing Up Mexican in America* by Margarita Longoria. As a person of color, I know firsthand how important it is for students to see themselves in the curricular content.

It is also important for us to not shrink from the trauma narrative of the community that we're talking about in our classrooms. We often see this when teachers only cover negative narratives about historically marginalized communities: enslavement, genocide, etc. So we need to also "center joy" in our classrooms. By this, I mean that educators need to focus on the happiness, resilience, and full humanity of our students and the histories that each person brings into the classroom.

Without this, we will perpetuate this trauma as the only narrative of the people from historically marginalized communities.

8 Christine Sleeter and Miguel Zavala, *Transformative Ethnic Studies in Schools: Curriculum, Pedagogy, and Research* (New York: Teachers College Press, 2020), 3.

9 Gholdy Muhammad, *Cultivating Genius: An Equity Framework for Culturally and Historically Responsive Literacy* (New York: Scholastic, 2020), 138.

This, in turn, shows students that they themselves are only capable of being a part of that trauma narrative, negatively impacting their sense of self.[10]

I center joy in my classroom by including literature written about people of color and authored by people of color, that is not focused on past injustices. Some pieces of literature that I use are *A Pho Love Story* by Loan Le; *The ABCs of Black History* by Rio Cortez and Lauren Semmer; *Firekeeper's Daughter* by Angeline Boulley; and *This Poison Heart* by Kaylnn Bayron. Each of these books provide students with different ways of seeing themselves and others through a lens that can help them feel seen and represented in our classroom through more than a single story.[11] I also have my students adorn our classroom walls with decorations that they believe represent themselves. When they create the decorations my only guidance for them is that it should be something that you feel represents who you are.

Some recent books I have found the most useful for creating a classroom where difficult conversations can happen are Dr. Gholdy Muhammad's *Cultivating Genius: An Equity Framework for Culturally and Historically Responsive Literacy*; Christine Sleeter and Miguel Zavala's *Transformative Ethnic Studies in Schools: Curriculum, Pedagogy, and Research*; and Tiffany Jewell's *This Book is Anti-Racist: 20 Lessons on How to Wake Up, Take Action, and Do the Work*. I've also used bits of *Cultivating Genius* and *This Book is Anti-Racist* with my students, because each book has valuable resources. I make sure to read each text beforehand and think about the conversations that could arise. Then I am better prepared, particularly for considerations of students who come from historically marginalized communities. This also helps me be mindful of what I want my students to get out of the lessons.

In lieu of reviewing the above, I would say that the best approach to difficult conversations in the classroom is to authentically listen to your students.

---

10 Sleeter and Zavala, *Transformative Ethnic Studies in Schools*, 45.

11 Chimamanda Ngozi Adichie, "The Danger of a Single Story," July 2009, video, 18:30, https://bit.ly/3jwOnzR.

Paul Cavanagh (he/him)

I am a fourth year English and Ethnic Studies teacher living in Tacoma, Washington, and I work at an alternative high school in the Franklin Pierce School District.

Before I begin, I should note that I am a cis-gendered, heterosexual white male who has experienced almost all of the privileges that our society unfairly bestows. My primary reason for stating this at the outset is because I believe critical self-reflection and openness about one's positionality are essential for any educator who engages in conversations about power, privilege, and the unadulterated history of the United States. Furthermore, these are conversations we need to be having in schools to help our students embrace their roles in dismantling systems of oppression and creating a more just and humane society for all.

If I couldn't acknowledge that much of the painful history of our country was deliberately hidden by white people to benefit white people, would my students (who look more like the people whose histories were deliberately excluded) want to learn from me, or trust me to facilitate such conversations? Would they feel comfortable being vulnerable in my classroom and asking honest questions and challenging the existing power structures?

Not a chance.

I believe our work as educators requires us to be brave, vulnerable, and loving toward all the students who walk into our classrooms. I learned this as a graduate student at the Evergreen State College in Washington. It was also there that I found that such an approach to education starts by looking in the mirror and trying to understand how your identity and background will impact the way students relate to you.

Here's what I mean: For me, I had to work to transform myself before I could think about transforming my classroom. This transformation began by discussing with peers and professors Maxine Greene's Teacher as Stranger, bell hooks' Teaching to

Transgress, and the ideas of Paulo Freire.[12] These texts provided me
with a framework for understanding the ways that power dynamics
in the larger society play out in our schools and classrooms. The
discourses I was able to have with professors and classmates
revealed to me that I had a responsibility to address and even
challenge these power dynamics in my classroom. To become this
teacher, which I'm still working on, I must be accountable for the
ways that power and privilege manifest in me regardless of my
well-meaning intentions. At times, my "white fragility," a term
coined by race scholar Robin DiAngelo, responded to this dynamic
defensively or with a sense of shame.[13] But I eventually learned that
I could condemn oppressive systems like white supremacy, class
privilege, and heteropatriarchy without condemning myself. What
is and was required was a transformation, a redefining of self as an
antiracist activist-educator dedicated to creating social and political
change inside and outside my classroom.

Greene argued that a teacher must "be moved to ask questions
about the universe, to engage in dialogue with [oneself] about the
world as it impinges on [them] and about the explanations others
provide."[14] I often wonder what my presence in the class brings
or allows for my students. Does it bring them closer to a more
equitable society?

Journalist, author, and historian Nikole Hannah-Jones was
recently asked whether *The 1619 Project* she developed would help
us gather around a more honest, unifying narrative of the country.[15]
This project is a major research effort by Hannah-Jones and other
writers at the *New York Times* and *New York Times Magazine*
to retell the story of America's history and founding with central

12 Specifically, Chapter 2 of Paulo Freire, *Pedagogy of the Oppressed: 50th Anniversary
Edition, trans. Myra Bergman Ramos* (New York: Bloomsbury Academic, 2018), 71–86,
which can be found online at: https://bit.ly/3rlMmuG.

13 Robin DiAngelo, *White Fragility: Why It's So Hard for White People to Talk About
Racism* (Boston: Beacon Press, 2018).

14 Maxine Greene, *Teacher as Stranger: Educational Philosophy for the Modern Age*
(Belmont, CA: Wadsworth, 1973), 21.

15 Nikole Hannah-Jones, "Nikole Hannah-Jones and the Country We Have," interview by
Rund Abdelfatah, Ramtin Arablouei, et al., Thoughtline, *NPR*, November 18, 2021, audio,
50:54, https://n.pr/37C3qpb. Also, for more information on "The 1619 Project,"

focus on the contributions of Black Americans.[16] Unsurprisingly, the endeavor has received fierce criticism from defenders of the false narrative of American exceptionalism and purity. In the interview, Hannah-Jones said that there is no single unifying narrative that exists about America, and that it is not up to the journalist to make that determination. The concern of a journalist, she says, "is to try to help us understand the society we live in and to get as close to the truth as possible."

That directly applies to the questions I ask myself about my role as a teacher. I am not there to spoon-feed "truth" to my students, but rather to be in partnership with them as seekers of truth. My task is to invite my students to look at the world critically and with curiosity, and then ask, "So what do you think?"

In the same interview, Hannah-Jones discussed the ways that history is continuously contested. The backlash to work like *The 1619 Project* comes out of a false sense that history has been settled, and anything new is a malicious attempt, as former president Donald Trump stated about the project, to rewrite "American history to teach our children that we were founded on the principle of oppression, not freedom."[17]

Many people, especially those who benefit from the traditional narrative of US history, are disturbed to find new interpretations on historical matters that were once thought settled. As educators, we must embrace the ever-changing nature of the histories that define us. This requires a prominent place in our curricula for voices that previously have been excluded from our classes and textbooks in an effort to hide the contributions and histories of Black, Brown, Indigenous, LGBTQIA+ people and communities. By including these stories, we can continuously engage in the process of transformation of self and society, and, by doing so, we will move toward a future where marginalized groups and perspectives are uplifted.

---

16 The 1619 Project, "The 1619 Project," *The New York Times Magazine* online, August 17, 2019, https://nyti.ms/3uzVhL5.

17 Katheryn Watson and Grace Sergers, "Trump Blasts 1619 Project on role of Black Americans and Proposes His Own '1776 commission'," CBS News, September 18, 2020, https://cbsn.ws/3xnlpKT.

As educators, we also need to center the voices of our students in our classrooms, schools, and communities. We must trust them, by which I mean trust that they can analyze and even create historically accurate accounts of history. If we don't elevate their voices, we perpetuate the harmful age-old myth that only some people and groups are worthy of being heard, and I can confidently say this does not align with my goal of educating for love and justice for all people and the planet.

Brooke Brown (she/her)

I've spent 15 years teaching English and ethnic studies at the high school level. I identify as a biracial Black woman who loves history and social justice, and I am passionate about providing spaces for healing and joy for all of my students daily. I am currently serving as a Teacher on Special Assignment as an Instructional Equity Specialist, merging equity and offering culturally responsive instruction throughout my district.

The poet and activist Sonya Renee Taylor (author of *The Body Is Not an Apology: The Power of Radical Self-Love*), offered the following observation on the importance of current events in 2020:

> We will not go back to normal. Normal never was. Our pre-corona existence was not normal other than we normalized greed, inequity, exhaustion, depletion, extraction, disconnection, confusion, rage, hoarding, hate and lack. We should not long to return, my friends. We are being given the opportunity to stitch a new garment. One that fits all of humanity and nature.[18]

One way for teachers to achieve Taylor's goal in class is to intentionally build community. To this end, I begin each class by setting the stage for what my students will be learning. We always start with a quote for or about an important social justice figure for

---

18 Sonya Renee Taylor (@sonyareneetaylor), "There Can Be No Going Back to 'Normal'," March 31, 2020, Instagram video, https://bit.ly/3KIElI0.

students to respond to.[19] I then present some slides on the person which includes a photo(s) of the person, biographical information, and the impact they have made on our world. I keep this presentation limited to two or three slides so I don't overwhelm the students. My goal is to spend no more than five minutes sharing, and I post these slides online so students have access to go back and learn more after class is over. It's important that students see historical figures who look like them as well as people who don't. This helps them view diversity as a strength.

In my classroom, it's imperative that students are introduced to concepts we call "mirrors, windows, and ladders." "Mirrors" are ways they can see themselves reflected in what we are learning about and studying. By providing opportunities for students to learn about their own history, mirrors develop their connection to the past, the land they come from, and their ancestors and culture. It can even develop and deepen their own self-love. For some students, exploring mirrors can be a journey of self-discovery and reclamation. For others, it is more of a celebration and validation.[20]

When we are in community with one another, we are more able to understand other perspectives and worldviews. That is why students also need "windows" into other people's lives. These help young people understand one another, and to learn about their peers' lived experiences, families, and cultures. Students can understand more about who they are, even as they see one another's humanity and develop compassion.

The "ladders" help students understand how society has been structured over time. A systemic understanding of our society is necessary for all of us to comprehend its past and present. A student's most important steps to reaching that understanding can be in their social studies classes. Understanding the ladder helps students to interrogate biases and stereotypes. As a young person, I sometimes took it personally when I was treated differently. I

---

19 Gretchen Brion-Meisels, Margaret Kavanagh, Thomas Nikundiwe, and Carla Shalaby, eds., *Planning to Change the World: A Plan Book for Social Justice Educators* (Education for Liberation Network, 2021), is a great resource to learn about incorporating social justice into your daily practice. It can be found at https://bit.ly/366Ik1V.

20 As educators, I believe we also need to take this journey ourselves beforehand so we are able to fully model it for our students.

thought there was something wrong with me. Having a wider understanding helps all students understand how systemic and institutional racism is "baked" into our society. Once we can see that, then we can work together to re-imagine a society that fits all students and has space for every single one of them to reach their full potential.

So, how do we begin? We all experienced trauma and discomfort during the pandemic. In that time, our students have not had adequate access to mental health professionals. Teachers had to try to check in and assess every student every day to make up the difference. My goal is also to help them develop the skills and capacity to care about one another. We often talk about how we're doing as a group, so after the social justice biographical slides, I project one that asks, "How you livin'?" My students then rate how they are feeling on that day. This helps me to look for patterns and understand how students are entering into the learning space. Keeping track like this also helps me to see if there are any dramatic shifts in the overall classroom mood.

After that, I project a "Get to know you" slide so that the young people in my classroom recognize that they are much more than just "students." Some days, this slide could ask something like, "What do you wish there was more of in the world?" On another day, "What is your favorite breakfast food?" I want my students to know that I care about their hopes and dreams, their likes and dislikes. They need to feel that I care about more than what they can produce in class; I care about their whole self. Then we learn about what events happened on this day in history. The Rethinking Schools planner has a great daily guide for teachers to consult and it also provides information about the event.[21] This helps students understand how the past is inextricably linked to our present, and it also can develop their critical understanding. Historicizing the present helps students understand how history has impacted what we are going through today.

---

21 This plan book for social justice educators can be found at rethinkingschools.org.

We then recite Luis Valdez's writing on In Lak'ech from his 1971 poem, "Pensamiento Serpentino," which my colleague Chance Las Dulce mentioned in his contributions to this chapter. The poem reads:

Tú eres mi otro yo	You are my other me.
Si te hago daño a ti	If I do harm to you,
Me hago daño a mi mismo	I do harm to myself;
Si te amo y respeto	If I love and respect
you,	
Me amo y respeto yo	I love and respect
myself.[22]	

Reading this together daily centers us as a class and reminds us that we are a learning community where all of our experiences are welcomed and valued and needed. We also talk about how this belief in interconnection is rooted in Indigenous culture and ensures there are no throwaway people. Everyone in our community is needed.

After this recitation, we do some deep breathing practices. (I just went through the 200-hour "Breathe for Change" wellness, SEL and Yoga teacher certification, which has helped so much.)[23] Most days, we begin by grounding ourselves in our environment and taking three deep breaths together. However, these practices change depending on the circumstances of the day. As a sign of the impact that practices like this can have, a student recently told me that although she experienced a panic attack for the first time, she was able to breathe through it because of the practices she developed in my class.

I am talking here about practices with students who I have established trust with. But how did I initiate these relationships? At the beginning of the school year, I spend at least the first week getting to know the students. I ask them to bring their "motto for life" to class as a first assignment. This could be a quote that they

---

22 Huerta, introduction to Luis Valdez, *Zoot Suit and Other Plays*, 10.

23 "200-hour Digital Wellness, SEL, and Yoga Teacher Training For Educators and Community Leaders," *Breathe for Change*, https://bit.ly/3vgr3vy.

feel represents their state of mind, or how they think, or a song lyric or pearl of wisdom from their aunty or grandmother. We then take turns sharing them in class. I always start to model for them and to show them they can do it as well. This is a low stakes way to have students introduce themselves and their perspectives to each other right off the bat!

We then spend a class period working on their lenses project. I keep the lights low by turning some of the classroom's fluorescent lights off. To add to the vibe, I've got strands of lights on around the room. I do this for a variety of reasons. Have you ever seen what happens when you take a poster off the wall? The wall is discolored and I often wonder if the lights do this to the wall, what are they doing to me? I also have noticed that keeping the lights low helps students have a sense of calm, with the atmosphere more like "home." Students share often about how they feel so comfortable in class and how they want to be there. They told me how they feel more ready to learn when they feel like they belong in the space.

In addition to the lighting, while we are working we listen to lo-fi hip-hop or electric violin. YouTube is a great place to listen to Chillhop, Josh Vietti, Black Violin, or my absolute favorite, Damien Escobar. It is an activity filled with music, coloring, giggling, and bonding that my students always remember fondly after they leave.

The next day, we sit in a big circle and share our lenses, and I always start. After all, how can we as teachers ask students to engage in work that is personal and uncomfortable if we are not doing it ourselves? In class, we listen intently to the presentations and show appreciation by snapping, just as if it were a spoken word session in a club. It usually takes two full days of class to get through presentations, because we are not in a rush at all. (For reference, I teach 12th grade and am teaching in a 55-minute class period.[24])

If lenses aren't your style, we've also done a variation of the activity and created "silhouettes" with one another. I divide my students into groups of three, we turn the lights off entirely, and I

24 I recently did this activity with Bill Gates! You can find it on his blog at: Bill Gates, "Can a Pair of Sunglasses Help Build Compassion In the Classroom?," *GatesNotes*, August 11, 2021, https://gatesnot.es/3E566HY.

instruct them to take out their cellphones. "Really?" they often ask. "Are you sure?" I assure them that this is for an exercise, which typically turns their curiosity into excitement. We then listen to lo-fi hip-hop or electric violin as the class takes turns tracing one another on butcher paper, cracking jokes, and building community. One person holds the cell phone with the flashlight on, one person stands with their face pressed sideways on the paper on the wall, and the third person traces. Once everyone has been traced, we spend anywhere from two to three days decorating our silhouettes. There's usually a big mess of magazines, markers, crayons, colored pencils, and paper those first few days, but it brings me joy. There is so much love and happiness to be found in such a mess.

To share out, we follow the same presentation process as we did for the "motto for life" activity. After students finish their silhouettes, we go around the class, share, and snap fingers in approval. Next, we display the completed works around the classroom. Each silhouette is proudly displayed on my back cabinets. By the end of this first week of school, we have gotten to know each other's personalities, humor, and creativity. We also have a better understanding of our values, because each person in the classroom has shared what is important to them and displayed it as an everyday reminder. If students join our class later in the year, I always have them do these projects as well so that they, too, can share who they are and be represented on our walls.

To build on this community, I have a two-day mini unit centered around poetry using "For My People" poems, which I first learned about from Linda Christensen in *Teaching for Joy and Justice*.[25] First, we study Margaret Walker's poem by listening to it read aloud and analyzing its messages.[26] Then I direct my students to write their own 20-line version of a "For My People" poem. In preparation for writing their original poems, we spend the next class period talking about what it's like to belong to a group, as well as the students' hopes and dreams. We then brainstorm the

---

25 Linda Christensen, *Teaching for Joy and Justice: Re-Imagining the Language Arts Classroom* (Milwaukee: Rethinking Schools, 2009), 27.

26 "For My People by Margaret Walker," February 10, 2015, video, 5:46, https://bit.ly/3jOuq7X.

different communities these young poets belong to and some of the things these groups unfairly face, including stereotypes. Then, they write their own poem about their people. Their homework is to finish writing their poem and be prepared to share it with the class the next day.

The following day, we get into a large circle, lower the lights— we do that a lot, as you may have noticed!—and then take turns reading our poems. I go first, and it always feels a little unsettling to be so vulnerable by sharing so much of my story so early into the year. Nevertheless, I must be a willing model for them.

Again, we go around and share, and after we finish, we snap. (I think there is something poetic, affirming, and community oriented about snapping over clapping. Maybe it's just me?) We then pass around a bucket where students contribute something positive about the poem they just heard: a golden line, or maybe something they identified with. It's up to them what they would like to share with the poem's writer. We spend about 2 minutes doing this after each person presents. We repeat this process for every student in the class, so everyone gets to hear something positive about their writing, their experience, and their identity from all their classmates. We need to have positive interactions before we have difficult ones, such as getting peer feedback on writing, or having a disagreement during a challenging conversation. It is so meaningful for them to hear positive affirmations so early on in the school year as we are building community. In fact, I often see those scraps of paper, cherished mementos of praise and validation from their classmates, saved in their notebooks when they present their senior portfolios at graduation.

After everyone has presented, I choose one line from each person's poem to create a class poem that I post in the back of the room near the lenses and silhouettes. Students can often be found standing around these projects in the back of the room, looking at them, touching them, reading them—I hear from so many students that these projects helped them feel less alone. I have also heard them say how much they have in common with peers they would never have known without doing this project. Students share so much from the heart in these poems. Some talk about immigrating to the United States. Others talk about the stress and pressures of high school, athletics, racism, sexism, or what it is like to come out to their parents and friends. High schoolers have a lot to share. Do we spend enough time in our classrooms asking them what they think?

I do all this in the first week of school with 12th graders each year to ensure that every one of my students understands that they are welcome to be themselves in our classroom. Together, we are working every day to create a brave, humanizing space where everyone can grow into their best selves. Individuality and a welcoming atmosphere helps foster belonging for students which helps them to be more engaged in the learning. For more on this, I suggest reading *Belonging Through a Culture of Dignity: The Keys to Successful Equity Implementation*, by Floyd Cobb and John Krownapple.[27]

Starting with low stakes but highly interesting discussions is a good way to open the pathway later for more difficult topics. So after we have spent time together, I initiate conversations on issues that resonate with them but are ultimately of relatively small consequence.

For example, I've found a surprisingly effective way to prepare young minds for such engagement: a class discussion on whether pineapple belongs anywhere near a pizza. My students take pizza seriously and will passionately defend their opinions on the subject. However, despite their differences, the undeniable appeal of pizza is enough for my students to respectfully disagree when choosing toppings. As students learn to respectfully disagree about pizza toppings, they are building their healthy disagreement muscles to have respectful discussions about more challenging topics. As a passionate pineapple-on-pizza lover, I can learn to respect those who would rather have mushrooms—gross—even though I would never agree.

Another excellent discussion point is to ask students the first time they learned about race. According to Anneliese Singh,

---

27 Floyd Cobb and John Krownapple, *Belonging Through a Culture of Dignity: The Keys to Successful Equity Implementation* (San Diego: Mimi & Todd Press, 2019).

the chief diversity officer and associate provost of diversity at Tulane University, developing a positive racial identity "entails nonjudgmental curiosity as you learn about your racial identity." Dr. Singh writes:

> Being curious about your race and racial identity development means that you question old ideas, remain open to new ones, and see what information best fits you—and you keep cultivating curiosity over time.[28]

This book is a great resource for teachers to consult to get conversations like these started. We use a compassionate listening protocol. The first step of the listening protocol is to pair the students off into a Partner 1 and a Partner 2. These partners are seated close together and face each other. Partner 1 then briefly talks about the first time they remember learning about race, while Partner 2 listens carefully. After three minutes, Partner 2 repeats Partner 1's experience back to them, summarizing what they consider to be its important elements. Partner 1 then adds anything omitted from the retelling that they feel was important to the story. Partner 2 can then share their experience, and the same process repeats. This experience provides a valuable lesson that, among other things, prioritizes student voice and respect for each other's time.

At this point, my classes are ready to have difficult conversations about race, oppression, and current events. But I can't emphasize enough how important it is for all students to understand that it is no single living person's fault for where we are today. Shame and blame do not belong in these challenging conversations.

It's also key for teachers to level with their students in order to have difficult discussions with them. Remember: You are not a "keeper" of knowledge. You are an educator, and the education you provide will be shaped by the experiences, wisdom, and talents

---

28 Anneliese A. Singh, *The Racial Healing Handbook: Practical Activities to Help You Challenge Privilege, Confront Systemic Racism, and Engage in Collective Healing* (Oakland, CA: New Harbinger Publications, 2019), 11.

that each student contributes to your classroom. As the teacher, I remind myself that I don't have to be perfect. I don't have to have it all together. I will make mistakes. I will apologize. And I will keep trying.

An important way I do so is by addressing dominant narratives and counter-narratives. Dominant narratives are the stories that society tells about how the status quo came to exist. These dominant narrative outlooks can be ubiquitous, disingenuous, and oppressive.[29] For example, the narrative that America is "the land of opportunity" makes it sound like everyone in the United States has an equal chance for economic and social mobility. This is not true today and most certainly was not true when James Truslow Adams, a wealthy white man and investment banker, first coined the term "the American dream" amid the Great Depression.[30]

Counter-narratives, in contrast, present narratives from different perspectives. They offer other sides to the story that have been left out, and reject the half-truths of a dominant narrative. But employing counter-narratives is not simply sharing multiple perspectives. It also means you have to study the context of a given time and place to understand the mindsets of varying perspectives.

One way to help teach about counter-narratives was to have students participate in a learning "mixer" on Rosa Parks, which is described in detail —complete with handouts —on the Zinn Education Project website.[31] The activity has students represent different aspects of Parks's life rather than lone figures. Of course, many high school students already know she was arrested for refusing to vacate her bus seat for a white passenger. However, few of my students identified her arrest as a catalyst for the 366-day Montgomery bus boycott, a watershed moment in the Civil Rights

29 Noreen Naseem Rodríguez and Katy Swalwell, *Social Studies for a Better World: An Anti-Oppressive Approach for Elementary Educators* (New York: W.W. Norton & Company Inc., 2022), 2–5.

30 Adams described "the American dream" in *The Epic of America* (Boston: Little, Brown, and Company, 1931) as "not a dream of motor cars and high wages merely, but a dream of social order in which each [person] shall be able to attain to the fullest stature of which they are innately capable, and be recognized by others for what they are, regardless ... of birth or position." For a detailed history of the expression's evolution and antecedents, see Jim Cullen, *The American Dream: A Short History of an Idea that Shaped a Nation* (New York: Oxford University Press, 2003).

31 Bill Bigelow, "The Rebellious Lives of Mrs. Rosa Parks," Zinn Education Project, 2020, https://bit.ly/3LY99oi.

Movement. None of my students knew Parks's rich history of social activism or her tense meeting with Dr. Martin Luther King Jr. to plan the boycott, which this activity can highlight. Each student was given a "new fact" about Parks and her life that they didn't know before. They went around the classroom and shared their facts and took notes. The "mixer" approach to sharing this information allows community learning, as opposed to a straightforward lesson on the topic. Students were so fascinated to learn about her life and wondered why they were just learning about this in 12th grade.

After our Parks mixer, I asked my students to research a historical event or phenomenon that interested them or connected to their own identity. Their goal: to present the dominant and counter-narrative of their chosen topics. This let my students combine the concepts they were studying with their own passions, which they then shared with their peers. The results were fantastic. As the student work came in, our classroom became a lyceum for excellent projects on flashpoints such as the Mauna Kea protests, the school-to-prison pipeline, missing and murdered Indigenous women, and racism in the medical system.

My students became young experts on their topics, which they then shared as "teacher" to their classmates. The students behave differently when they understand that they are all responsible for each other's learning, aid, and focus. This forms an interdependence that encourages empathy and empowered learners.

A word of caution: Not all mixers are good experiences for students, and some mixers can actually cause harm if not conducted thoughtfully. Do not have students act out oppression through role-play or simulations in which they marginalize each other, even if they say they would like to.

A great way to teach about racism and oppression is through John Bell's "Four I's of Oppression."[32] Bell identifies these I's as Ideological, Institutional, Interpersonal, and Internalized.

---

32 R. Tolteka Cuauhtin, "Teaching John Bell's Four I's of Oppression," in R. Tolteka Cuauhtin, Miguel Zavala, Christine Sleeter, and Wayne Au, eds., *Rethinking Ethnic Studies* (Milwaukee: Rethinking Schools, 2019), 216–219.

I would like to close by sharing that Native American teacher and writer R. Tolteka Cuauhtin reminds us that "providing a framework and language for students is very helpful in moving from an experiential level of oppression to a conceptual analysis as part of their empowerment." You can provide opportunities to do just that in your social studies classroom.

Julien Pollard

I am an Afro-Hawaiian educator born, raised, living, and working in Tacoma, Washington. My first three years in education were as a high school counselor and I am now in my second year as the Equity Coordinator in the central office helping steward the district's vision toward a more humanizing experience for our students, staff, and community.

My contributions to this conversation are grounded in the reflexive work and systemic efforts that support teacher practices. In my professional experience, it is much more difficult to be a critical, antiracist, liberatory educator than not. This country was founded on the genocide of Indigenous tribes, enslavement of Africans, and the exploitation of people from across the globe. So it follows that educators in US schools would experience challenges as they identify and dismantle the legacies of injustice in our system. For some teachers, this difficulty might be defined by social and professional isolation within their school, a lack of support from the administration or community, and the ongoing politicization of counter-narratives to American exceptionalism.

To counteract this, I try to hold myself to two principles:

1. Objectivity is a myth.
2. Neutrality reinforces the status quo.

James Baldwin tell us that, "You can not describe anything without betraying your point of view, your aspirations, your fears, your hopes."[33] What we teach and how we teach it communicates

33 James Baldwin, "James Baldwin: Looking Towards the Eighties," interview by Kalamu ya Salaam, The Black Collegian, no. 10 (1979): 105–110, in *Conversations with James Baldwin*, eds. Fred L. Standley and Louis H. Pratt (Jackson: University Press of Mississippi, 1989), 180.

our values. What is sometimes understood as objective truth is often just a normalization of our country's capitalist white cis-heterosexual values. Furthermore, people who challenge oppressive systems are nearly always met with resistance. So prepare yourself for pushback!

I have found that my community is my greatest resource in this respect. I believe most people want a free and just world. Oppression and injustice thrive when freedom dreamers are isolated. In my practice, I take calculated risks when I speak out. I do so knowing that there may be another person hearing me who is prepared to claim or reclaim their voice in their own pursuit of justice. That person needs to know they are not alone.

Social justice work is the most difficult but affirming work I ever have undertaken. I have experienced how there are few moments more discouraging than when the system resists reform. So I have joined a community of "freedom fighters" who host weekly meetings. At these, we exchange feedback on projects, share family updates, encourage each other to lead balanced lives, and hold each other accountable. One of my greatest influences in this endeavor has been the organizer, educator, and writer, Mariame Kaba. In her book, *We Do This 'til We Free Us*, Kaba writes that "Hope is a discipline." The community of freedom fighters offers me the perspective to continue on when I feel despair. Hope is a discipline, and it helps if it's shared.

If we hope to cultivate classrooms where difficult conversations can occur, then we must practice justice and liberation in every facet of our lives. My work continually revisits my beliefs and how they impact my interactions with others. For me, this involves a lot of education, research, reading, and ongoing awareness. It means demonstrating trustworthiness and openness to others so that I receive honest feedback from them when I show up outside of my values. And it also means making a commitment to dismantle a society that has rewarded me for much of my life for upholding the status quo.

While it's an obvious thing to point out, our society shapes us. So in a capitalist society that prioritizes output and resources, I might ask: How does capitalism shape my beliefs? Do I engage with students differently because they produce certain grades and test scores? We live in a society that has normalized putting human beings in cages as punishment for breaking a law. How does this practice shape my response to a student who steals property off my desk? Even further, what is justice and accountability in a society where a young person feels that is their best option? In a society that necessitates inequality, grappling with how our beliefs have been shaped by the logics of those systems is our first step toward a more just world.

As educators, having difficult conversations begins with *our* learning: what we teach, what we've been taught, and what we still have to learn. Students are already having these conversations. Adults need to facilitate and empower these dialogues with environments that are inclusive, respectful, and dignified for all. We must also look beyond our schools to our entire society, for we will always need new garments more befitting humanity and nature, which is ever-changing. Our kids are waiting and watching us. I believe in you, and I believe in us. The world we leave behind is a legacy that defines the type of ancestor we can be. We should remind ourselves of whose shoulders we stand on and who paved the way for us to be here today. How can we best honor their legacies and sacrifices? With a world that all young people belong in and will preserve. Let's work together to build it for them!

Brooke Brown, 2021 Washington Teacher of the Year, has spent 15 years teaching English and ethnic studies at the high school level. She loves history and social justice, and is passionate about providing spaces for healing and joy for all of her students each day. She is currently serving as a teacher on special assignment as an instructional equity specialist at Washington High School in Washington, merging equity and offering culturally responsive instruction throughout her district.

Kim Bond has worked in education for 7 years and has spent the past 3 as a classroom teacher at the middle level. She currently teaches eighth-grade English language arts in Parkland, Washington.

Paul Cavanagh is in his fourth year teaching English and Ethnic Studies in Tacoma, Washington. He works at an alternative high school in the Franklin Pierce School District.

Chance Las Dulce has been an educator for the past 7 years at the elementary, middle, and high school levels. He currently teaches high school English and Ethnic Studies in Tacoma, Washington.

Julien Pollard is an educator born, raised, living, and working in Tacoma, Washington. He started his career as a high school counselor. He is currently in his second year as the equity coordinator, helping steward his district's vision toward a more humanizing experience for the students, staff, and community.

Matt Price is in his seventh year as an educator at the high school level. He currently teaches Environmental Science and Food Justice in Tacoma, Washington, on the land of the spuyaləpabš (the Puyallup Nation) and the Coast Salish Peoples.

IN CLOSING

It is self-evident, yet bears repeating: Social studies teachers are absolutely essential for our nation, and they carry even greater importance when democracy is threatened. A government of the people and by the people requires an educated and active citizenry to ensure their government functions for the people.

In other words, the United States needs good social studies teachers now more than ever.

Hot Button's contributors have shared some of the same professional and personal expectations, hardships, and dilemmas faced by social studies teachers across this country. Taken as a whole, their work raises the question: When was the last time in US history that so much anger was directed against our schools?

An argument could be made that it was after the *Brown v. Board of Education* school desegregation decision in 1954. The years that followed were no doubt daunting and explosive times to teach students about their history and liberties. So much of both had been denied to so many. So we acknowledge and thank those educators of yesteryear.

We also extend that same profound thanks to today's social studies teachers, who risk their health and safety to preserve our notion of nation. Their work confronting issues like racism, parental choice, and disinformation has required extraordinary preparation, patience, and courage.

We at Gibbs Smith Education are here to help these educators, and we look forward to working with them to share more strategies and tools for authentic social studies instruction in all classrooms in the future.

APPENDIX

To accompany the essays in this book, the authors and editors of *Hot Button* have included the following images and documents as supplemental materials.

I. From "Insurrection Nation: Teaching about Domestic Terrorism in Real Time," Alysha Butler-Arnold
   - The First Colored Senator and Representatives, Currier & Ives (1872)
   - Colored Rule in a Reconstructed(?) State, Thomas Nast (1872)
   - "Legislative and Administrative Actions Regarding CRT" (November 21, 2021)
II. From "Primary Considerations: Navigating Sensitive History with Younger Students," Kelly Reichardt
   - "Sensory Figure" handout
   - "S.I.T. and Think" handout
   - Recommended readings
III. From: "Shared Perspectives: Empowering Classroom Communities for Important Conversations," Brooke Brown
   - Resources
   - Lenses template

All other material shared or referenced in this text may be found via footnotes. For further inquiry, feel free to contact this book's editors at Gibbs Smith Education.

Appendix I

FROM: "Insurrection Nation: Teaching about Domestic Terrorism in Real Time" by Alysha Butler-Arnold

The First Colored Senator and Representatives, by Currier & Ives (1872)[1]

Colored Rule in a Reconstructed(?) State, by Thomas Nast (1872)[2]

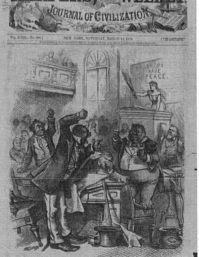

---

1 Currier & Ives, *The First Colored Senator and Representatives, in the 41st and 42nd Congress of the United States*, lithograph, 1872, from Library of Congress Prints and Photographs Division, https://www.loc.gov/resource/ppmsca.17564.

2 Thomas Nast, *Colored Rule in a Reconstructed(?) State*, *Harper's Weekly*, March 14, 1874, p. 229, Library of Congress Prints and Photographs Division, https://www.loc.gov/item/91705051/.

"Legislative and Administrative Actions Regarding CRT"[3]

Successful bans by legislatures	
Arizona	House Bill 2898, which was signed by Gov. Doug Ducey on 6/30/21, prohibited the use of "public monies for instruction that presents any form of blame or judgment on the basis of race, ethnicity or sex" in K-12 public/charter schools and establishes fines for violations. However, on 11/2/21 the Arizona Supreme Court upheld a trial court ruling that HB2898 violates the state constitution by including multiple subjects in a single bill, and it was invalidated. See the Arizona Board of Education guidance here.
Idaho	House Bill 377, which was signed by Gov. Brad Little on 4/28/21, bans teaching specified concepts about race and gender in public schools, public charter schools, and public institutions of higher education.
Iowa	House File 802, which was signed by Gov. Kim Reynolds on 6/8/21, bans incorporating specified concepts regarding race and sex into mandatory trainings for government agencies, teachers, and higher education students. Specified concepts must also not be included in curriculum in public K-12 schools.
New Hampshire	Anti-CRT section was incorporated into House Bill 2, the state budget trailer, and signed by Gov. Chris Sununu on 6/25/21. This bill prohibits teaching specified concepts in public schools and in governmental agency trainings.
North Dakota	House Bill 1508, which was signed by Gov. Doug Burgum on 11/15/21, prohibits K-12 public schools from instruction related to critical race theory, which is defined in the bill as the "that racism is systemically embedded in American society and the American legal system to facilitate racial inequality."
Oklahoma	House Bill 1775, which was signed by Gov. Kevin Stitt on 5/7/21, prohibits public institutions of higher education from requiring students to participate in mandatory gender/sexuality diversity training, and bans teaching specified concepts about race and sex in public schools. The Oklahoma Department of Education elaborated here about how the law will operate, including reporting violations.
South Carolina	Anti-CRT section incorporated into the education section of H. 4100, the state budget bill, which was passed on 6/30/21. This bill prohibits schools receiving state funding from teaching specified concepts regarding race and sex.
Tennessee	House Bill 580, which was signed by Governor Lee on 5/25/21, bans public school districts and public charter schools from teaching certain concepts about race, sex, and the United States, withholds state funding for violations. The Tennessee State Department of Education details these rules and the complaint system here.
Texas	House Bill 3979 (signed into law on 6/15/21) was replaced with stricter legislation, Senate Bill 3 (signed into law on 9/17/21). SB3 makes significant changes to required civics education curriculum, establishes a new civics training program for teachers, requires that both sides of current controversial issues are presented, prohibits teaching certain concepts regarding race and sex and giving academic credit for advocacy work.

3 Rashawn Ray and Alexandra Gibbons, "Why Are States Banning Critical Race Theory?" *Brookings Institution*, November 2021, https://www.brookings.edu/blog/fixgov/2021/07/02/why-are-states-banning-critical-race-theory.

State legislatures that have/are considering a ban or that have pre-filed bills for next session	
Alabama	Two bills have been pre-filed for the next legislative session: • HB8 would limit the concepts about race and sex that public schools and universities can teach • HB11 would require public schools and universities to terminate employees that teach certain concepts about race and sex
Alaska	• Rep. Thomas McKay (R) pre-filed a bill that would ban teaching certain concepts about race and sex and ban the 1619 Project
Arkansas	• Senate Bill 627 passed. It limits how most state agencies can train employees about "divisive concepts" • Bills limiting how racism is taught in schools (HB1218) and banning the 1619 project in schools (HB1231) have failed thus far
Florida	Although the BOE already passed new rules regarding teaching about race and gender, additional legislation (HB57) has been pre-filed that would dictate how concepts related to race and gender are taught at K-12 public schools, public universities, state colleges, state agencies, local governments, and private businesses with state/local government contracts
Kentucky	Two bills have been pre-filed for the next legislative session: • BR 60 would ban certain concepts from being taught in public K-12 schools and establish financial penalties for disobeying. It also bans mandatory diversity training at public universities. • BR 69 would ban concepts from being taught both in public K-12 schools and in public universities; institutions that disobey would be legally liable.
Louisiana	House Bill 564 would ban "divisive concepts" from being taught in public schools and public postsecondary institutions, but it has been deferred for now
Maine	HP 395 would ban certain subjects/concepts regarding race and gender from being taught in public schools
Michigan	• Senate Bill 460 would ban (and withhold 5% of state funding to districts who do not cooperate) the teaching of the 1619 Project and specified concepts regarding race and gender in K-12 public and charter schools • House Bill 5097, which passed the House in November 2021, would ban specified concepts regarding race and gender from being included in the core curriculum standards set by the State Board of Education and local school districts
Mississippi	• House Resolution 62 and Senate Resolution 56 condemn critical race theory but do not address schools specifically • In the FY23 Executive Budget Recommendation, Governor Reeves urges legislators to pass an anti-CRT bill and proposes a "$3 million investment in a Patriotic Education Fund"
Missouri	House Bill 952 would ban certain concepts from being taught in state agencies, school districts, public postsecondary institutions, and state-funded charter schools, including specified curriculum (1619 Project, Learning for Justice Curriculum by SPLC, We Stories, programs by Educational Equity Consultants, BLM at School, Teaching for Change, Zinn Education Project). State funding would be withheld from entities who violate these rules.

New Jersey	S-4166 would prohibit specified concepts from being taught in public schools, mandate teachers to present "materials supporting both sides of a controversial issue [an issue that is part of an electoral party platform]"and require the State Board of Education to introduce rules prohibiting political advocacy in the classroom
New York	A8253 would ban Regents and school districts in New York from establishing curriculum that teaches specified concepts related to race and from teaching the 1619 Project
North Carolina	House Bill 324 would ban certain concepts from being taught in public schools and charter schools; it passed the state House and Senate but was vetoed in September by Gov. Cooper
Ohio	• House Bill 322 states that teachers who discuss current events must introduce multiple perspectives, bans extra credit for political advocacy work, bans private funding for curriculum deemed unacceptable by bill, bans state agencies and school districts from teaching certain concepts • House Bill 327 would ban school districts and state agencies from teaching various "divisive concepts," would withhold state funding to districts that disobeyed
Pennsylvania	House Bill 1532 would ban public postsecondary institutions, state and local governments, and school districts from teaching certain concepts, a violation would result in a loss of state funding
Rhode Island	H 6070 would prohibit teaching of "divisive concepts" in schools, state and municipal contracts and training programs
West Virginia	• House Bill 2595 would ban state employees or contractors, as well as schools, from teaching "divisive concepts" and would withhold state funding for violations • Senate Bill 618 would ban the State Board of Education from implementing curriculum that promotes "divisive concepts" and "critical race theory" and allows for the firing of teachers who teach certain concepts related to race and gender
Wisconsin	• Senate Bill 411 would prohibit certain concepts from being taught in public schools and charter schools, with violations resulting in a loss of 10% of state funding. Also requires curricula used to be posted online. • Senate Bill 410 would restrict the types of racism/sexism training that state agencies can conduct • Senate Bill 409 would ban certain concepts from being taught in University of Wisconsin System and the Technical College System and restricts permissible employee training, with violations resulting in funding cuts
Wyoming	State Senators plan to introduce the "Civics Transparency Act" would require school districts to post learning materials and activities used in the preceding year

Federal-level action being considered

- The "Saving History Act of 2021" would withhold federal funding, with some exceptions, from schools that teach the 1619 Project.

- The "Ending Critical Race Theory in D.C. Public Schools Act," introduced by a representative from Wisconsin, would ban certain concepts from being taught in D.C. public and charter schools.

- The "Stop CRT Act" would withhold federal funding from schools and universities that promote "race-based theories."

- The Senate passed an amendment to the budget resolution with Manchin's support blocking federal funding from being used to teach CRT in pre-K and K-12 schools.

- The "PEACE Act" would prohibit federal American History and civics education programming funds from being used to teach "divisive concepts."

- The "Protecting Students from Racial Hostility Act" would amend Title VI of the Civil Rights Act of 1964 to make the teaching of "divisive concepts" discriminatory, establishes a system for reporting related complaints.

Appendix II

FROM: "Primary Considerations: Navigating Sensitive History with Younger Students," Kelly Reichardt

Sensory Figure

Complete this activity by answering these statements from the perspective of the athlete. Consider their personality and passion too!

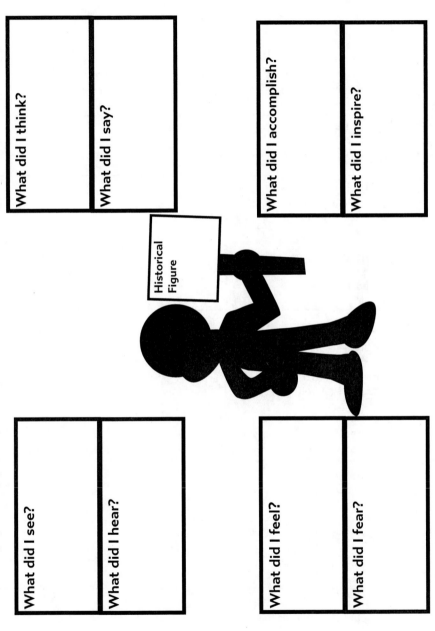

| What did I think? |
| What did I say? |

| What did I accomplish? |
| What did I inspire? |

Historical Figure

| What did I see? |
| What did I hear? |

| What did I feel? |
| What did I fear? |

Graphic by Kelly Reichardt and Jackson Reichardt.

S.I.T. and Think²

Investigate each source. Capture your observations in this graphic organizer.

Source #:	Caption/Title:
Surprising: What did you observe that you didn't expect?	
Interesting: What did you find noteworthy?	
Troubling: What was concerning or uncomfortable?	
Think: What do you think the enslaver felt about the enslaved person that sought their freedom?	
Think: How do you think the public reacted to this broadside? How did you react to it?	

Source #:	Caption/Title:
Surprising: What did you observe that you didn't expect?	
Interesting: What did you find noteworthy?	
Troubling: What was concerning or uncomfortable?	
Think: What do you think the enslaver felt about the enslaved person that sought their freedom?	
Think: How do you think the public reacted to this broadside? How did you react to it?	

Template by Kelly Reichardt and Jackson Reichardt.

Recommended Readings

Fox, Mem. *Whoever You Are*. New York: Voyager Books, 1997.

Frank, Anne. *Anne Frank: The Diary of a Young Girl*. New York: Doubleday & Company, 1952.

Hannah-Jones, Nikole and Renée Watson. *The 1619 Project: Born on Water*. New York: Kokila, 2021.

Jiang, Ji-li. *Red Scarf Girl: A Memoir of the Cultural Revolution*. New York: HarperTrophy, 1997.

Noah, Trevor. *It's Trevor Noah, Born a Crime: Adapted for Young Readers*. New York: Delacorte Press, 2019.

Schroff, Laura and Alex Tresniowski. *An Invisible Thread: The True Story of an 11-Year-Old Panhandler, a Busy Sales Executive, and an Unlikely Meeting with Destiny*. New York: Howard Books, 2011.

Spiegelman, Art. *The Complete Maus: A Survivor's Tale*. New York: Pantheon, 2011.

Appendix III

FROM: "Shared Perspectives: Empowering Classroom Communities for Important Conversations" by Brooke Brown.

Resources

Affaf, Sameen. "You Cannot Bring About What You Are Not." August 12, 2021. Instagram. https://www.instagram.com/sameen.affaf/?hl=en.

Agarwal-Rangnath, Ruchi. *Planting the Seeds of Equity: Ethnic Studies and Social Justice in the K–2 Classroom*. New York: Teachers College Press, 2020.

Au, Wayne, Anthony L. Brown, and Dolores Aramoni Calderón. *Reclaiming the Multicultural Roots of U.S. Curriculum: Communities of Color and Official Knowledge in Education*. New York: Teachers College Press, 2016.

Duncan-Andrade, Jeffrey M.R. and Ernest Morrell. *The Art of Critical Pedagogy: Possibilities for Moving from Theory to Practice in Urban Schools*. Bern, Switzerland: Peter Lang, 2008.

Eagle Shield, Alayna, Django Paris, Rae Paris, and Timothy San Pedro, eds. *Education in Movement Spaces: Standing Rock to Chicago Freedom Square*. Oxfordshire, UK: Routledge, 2020.

German, Lorena Escoto. *Textured Teaching: A Framework for Culturally Sustaining Practices*. Portsmouth, NH: Heinemann, 2021.

Ladson-Billings, Gloria. *The Dreamkeepers: Successful Teachers of African American Children*. San Francisco: Jossey-Bass, 1994.

Ladson-Billings, Gloria. *Culturally Relevant Pedagogy: Asking a Different Question*. New York: Teachers College Press, 2021.

Love, Bettina L., Jay Gillen, and Mariame Kaba. *Lessons in Liberation: An Abolitionist Toolkit for Educators*. Oakland, CA: AK Press, 2021.

Lysicott, Jamila. *Black Appetite. White Food. Issues of Race, Voice, and Justice Within and Beyond the Classroom*. Oxfordshire, UK: Routledge, 2019.

Marsh, Tyson E.J. and Natasha N. Croom, eds. *Envisioning a Critical Race Praxis in K–12 Education Through Counter-Storytelling*. Charlotte, NC: Information Age Publishing, 2016.

Minor, Cornelius. *We Got This: Equity, Access, and the Quest to Be Who Our Students Need Us to Be*. Portsmouth, NH: Heinemann, 2019.

Muhammad, Gholdy. Cultivating Genius: *An Equity Framework for Culturally and Historically Responsive Literacy*. New York: Scholastic, 2020.

Paris, Django and H. Samy Alim, eds. *Culturally Sustaining Pedagogies: Teaching and Learning for Justice in a Changing World*. New York: Teachers College Press, 2017.

Stembridge, Adeyemi. *Culturally Responsive Education in the Classroom: An Equity Framework for Pedagogy*. Oxfordshire, UK: Routledge, 2019.

Tuhiwai Smith, Linda, Eve Tuck, and K. Wayne Yang, eds. *Indigenous and Decolonizing Studies in Education*. Oxfordshire, UK: Routledge, 2019.

Lenses Template (courtesy Brooke Brown and Gates Venture)